MONEY MAGIC

MONEY MAGIC

Practical Wisdom and Empowering Rituals to HEAL YOUR FINANCES

by **THE MONEY WITCH**

Jessie Susannah Karnatz

Art by Broobs

CHRONICLE BOOKS
SAN FRANCISCO

Library of Congress Cataloging-in-Publication Data
Names: Karnatz, Jessie Susannah, author.
Title: Money magic : practical wisdom and empowering rituals to heal your
    finances / by Jessie Susannah Karnatz, the Money Witch ; art by Broobs.
Description: San Francisco : Chronicle Books, [2021]
Identifiers: LCCN 2021019746 | ISBN 9781797210353 (hardcover)
Subjects: LCSH: Finance, Personal. | Money.
Classification: LCC HG179 .K35 2021 | DDC 332.024—dc23
LC record available at https://lccn.loc.gov/2021019746

Manufactured in China.

Design by Allison Weiner.
Art by Broobs.
Typesetting by Frank Brayton.

10 9 8 7 6 5 4 3

Chronicle books and gifts are available at special quantity discounts to
corporations, professional associations, literacy programs, and other
organizations. For details and discount information, please contact our
premiums department at corporatesales@chroniclebooks.com or at
1-800-759-0190.

Chronicle Books LLC
680 Second Street
San Francisco, California 94107
www.chroniclebooks.com

This book is dedicated to G-d, for guiding me on my path and inviting me to do this work in the human world.

To the ancestors and the descendants. May this work be a blessing that heals throughout time and space.

And to Hermes Mercury, the best bad-boy boyfriend a business babe could ever want.

CONTENTS

Step 2: Stop Being Polite and Start Getting Real

Ground in self-awareness through an accurate assessment of your behaviors, feelings, and opinions about money.

54

Step 3: Figure Out What You Want, What You Really, Really Want

Identify your true financial desires, and then refine them into real-life goals.

78

Step 7: Try.
Definitely Fail. Try Again.

*Cocreate with the Universe by aligning
your actions with your intentions.*

180

Getting Closure
201

Thank-Yous
205

A LOVE LETTER FROM THE MONEY WITCH

I f handling our finances were as easy as just doing what it says on the blogs, we'd already be doing it. But the truth is, most of us are out here confused and ashamed because we didn't pay down $80,000 of student loans in three years, we haven't bought a house, and we're not raking in six figures from our side hustle. If you are making good money, you're likely hustling so hard that you barely have time to keep track of your sanity, much less your checking account. It might feel as if you have nothing to show for how far you've come and all the efforts you've made. Maybe you're holding the secret shame that you haven't filed your taxes in two years and you're constantly worried the IRS is going to show up on your doorstep (Spoiler alert: They won't). Maybe you're low-key terrified to make a budget because you don't even want to know how much you spend on food delivery each month. Seeing those numbers brings up shame about not only our finances but also our body image issues, which then brings up our fear that we'll never be partnered, which then brings up our issues with our mom and . . . actually, I'm just gonna take an edible and watch TV.

Deep breath. You are not alone. This stuff is normal. It's normal to feel overwhelmed and underprepared for the financial realities of adulthood. It's normal to feel panicked by money. It's normal to let fear turn into avoidance, and to let avoidance turn into denial. I've been there, sometimes I'm still there, and we're going to get through this together.

You deserve this book. You deserve accessible, spiritually aware, culturally affirming financial information. You deserve to feel confident when navigating the financial world.

I am not going to pretend to be able to meet you in every part of your experience and identity, but I can promise you I don't sound like a banker, and I don't sound like your dad getting mad at you for not taking his advice. I sound more like if finance maven Suze Orman took psychedelic mushrooms.

I've seen the underbelly of a lot of people's finances, and believe me, you're not the messiest mess around. Your situation isn't shocking or appalling—and even if it is, I'm not here to shame you. You've got under-the-table income, a shopping bag full of unopened letters from the IRS stashed in a closet, and credit card debt you're hiding from your partner? I understand how it can get like that. It doesn't matter where you are financially at this moment: It's never too late to make a comeback; every one of us can benefit from looking under the hood of our finances. You may have arrived here unprepared, but it's not too late to learn how to do this.

————

In this very moment, you can declare, "I am ready for my finances to be different, I am ready to be healed."

————

A lot of us block out financial information and education that might help us succeed because the delivery isn't appealing or, on a deeper level, it's even triggering. We want easier financial lives, to struggle less with money and adulting, but it seems like a tedious, insurmountable task. In my thirteen years working in financial education, I've repeatedly noticed that a lot of the tools meant to empower us just seem ugly and boring, not to mention super intimidating. (I've always thought a Hello Kitty bookkeeping app would make a killing.)

When the tedium shifts to a deeper layer of dread and trigger, then we really tune out—and things spiral out from there. That's what most financial education gets wrong—it doesn't hold us as the emotional, complex, sometimes messy beings that we are. It doesn't touch on all the dimensions that sensitive, intuitive people navigate as part of our daily existence. When we talk about money, we're not just talking about salaries and bank accounts and budgeting; we're also activating a whole web of connected thought-feelings. When we don't get to name everything else that's in the room with us, we start to feel uncomfortable, alienated, and like we're straight up just not having a good time. And when I say there are other things in the room—it's a packed house! Every time we look at our bank account or pay a bill, we bring along our relationship to and experience of self-worth, societal value, gender, colonialism, racialization, migration, family trauma, abuse history, education, family of origin expectations, assimilation, survival and our ancestors' survival, childhood, divorce, dis/ability . . . like, every damn thing.

You are showing up as a multidimensional being to your financial life, just like you do to every part of your life, and I want to provide you with a financial framework that can meet you in your entirety. We are sensitive, gorgeous, aware, conscious babes who want ease for ourselves but also for all people of Earth, and for the Earth itself. The financial world is largely shaped by privileged members of older generations, leaving so many others feeling alienated and like we have to abandon our values and conform to inauthentic ways of operating in order to achieve stability. We need to talk about money and how to be successful in a way that sees the whole truth and pokes holes in the mythology of capitalism.

Every year more and more of us are reconnecting to a multidimensional reality—one that holds the political, the spiritual, the emotional—honoring our ancestral practices and leaning into a liberatory future. As we face the obligations and challenges of becoming citizens of the world we want to live in, the mandate to heal all areas of our lives becomes super essential. We need to find our way toward a visionary relationship to our finances.

This is a book about how to do your best to thrive financially in a holistic way that incorporates your sensitivity, your creativity, and your integrity. This book respects distrust and dislike for capitalism. This book thinks that what you want and how you feel matter. This book holds the interconnectedness of us all. I'm not going to spend a lot of time telling you what to do, but I am going to help you see for yourself how your core wounds pop up to influence and sometimes sabotage your financial life.

Naming the emotions that are connected to our finances is not an aside, something to indulge in once we figure out the logistical pieces. It is the key to practical material success.

Understanding your emotional relationship to money is the answer to all the "why can't I seem to . . ." financial questions that haunt your self-esteem. The answer is inside you, inside this web of feelings and reactions that gets lit up when you interact with money. Acknowledging, validating, naming, and understanding this web is what is going to take you to the next level.

So let me say, I am really honored to be here with y'all. Many of us are hurting financially but can't seem to heal this part of our lives. Thank you for seeking, thank you for not giving up, thank you for picking up this book and giving it one more try. I honor your labor in showing up for yourself, for this piece of #boringselfcare. Thank you for allowing me to participate in your process around money. I know it's deep in here, and scary, and intimate, and I hold dearly the trust you put in me by letting me in to talk to you. By picking up this book, you're already doing the work to show up for yourself. I am going to do the work of making sure you get treated with the care and respect and trust you deserve.

You are the authority on your own life. But when it comes to money, it's easy to get confused and forget that we know what's best for us. I want to help you understand how to embody that authority, that sovereignty, when facing your finances. Your financial self-esteem is essential.

I love you, I trust you, and I believe in you. The work of healing your finances is the work of healing everything in your life. So let's get into it.

"Or, do whatever you want!"

xoxo
Money Witch

The

MONEY WITCH

PHILOSOPHY

OF HEALING

A foundation for
making money magic

BECOMING
THE MONEY WITCH

The question I get asked the most is how I became the Money Witch, and whether I figured out all my own money issues before I started coaching. Story time!

In 2012, I was a divorcing, newly evicted, almost-full-time single parent to a three-year-old. My ex had just started their first ever professional job and was sharing their salary with me, but it was not sustainable for either of us financially or emotionally. I had no car, and I hadn't formally worked outside of the home in more than three years, since my first attempt at starting a financial business had completely fallen apart. Most of my work experience was in strip clubs or restaurants. I had no college degree. To make matters worse, I was in a very painful relationship and was experiencing emotional abuse. I was all the way fucked up.

I tried to get a job performing at the Lusty Lady, a unionized, worker-cooperatized peep show in San Francisco. It seemed like a guaranteed way to make some money while I figured things out. I'd worked there for a substantial part of my twenties, finally quitting when I was too pregnant to wobble around on stilettos any longer. I had to eat my pride to even try to get a job dancing there again, as when I left I had been the lead madam, a.k.a. head dancer manager. I mean, I had been on the founding board of directors of the worker cooperative. The person who was managing at the time was someone I had hired and trained as a dancer, but she required me to come in, fill out an application, and wait to dance on stage just like all the other applicants.

I call what happened next "G-d hit me in the ankle with a golf club." I was walking to the dressing room to get changed, and on flat ground, in flat sneakers, I twisted my ankle so badly that I fell to the floor crying. I was so angry and embarrassed. I had traversed this same spot literally thousands of times in six-inch lucite heels and never even stumbled. Needless to say, going back to dancing was no longer an option. I wouldn't be able to wear heels for the next six years.

I went back to the drawing board, wrote a résumé, and applied for an executive assistant job at a nonprofit for sex workers in the city, headed by people I knew. I was not hired. I began selling margaritas and joints in Dolores Park with one of my best friends on the weekends. We were making good money. After a few months of being able to rely on this steady income, we got aggressively arrested. To this day, I'm not sure why we got singled out, as every time I go back to the park, there's the same roaming vendors who have been there for years—the rum-in-a-coconut pirate dude, the hottie with the weed truffles in a copper pot. We tried to go back to selling a month or so later, during Pride, and just as we were entering the park, a police officer stopped us and made us pour three liters of tequila on the ground.

It was clear that my life as a freelance controlled-substance distributor wasn't going to work out, and I began to think about what skills I had to start a new business on my own. I'd previously cofounded a bookkeeping, tax prep, and financial coaching business with a friend in 2008, called Brass Tacks: Purveyors of Radical Effectiveness. I'd taken the HR and business management skills I had developed at the Lusty Lady and started training in the finances side under my business partner and through City College of San Francisco courses. We catered to the worker-cooperative community with a cute vintage feminist aesthetic. Our branding was impeccable! Four months after our epically fashionable office-warming party, our friendship, and then our business, folded. I had been dealing with extreme pregnancy-related illness, and ultimately an incompatible business partnership just did us in. But I kept doing a bit of taxes, book-keeping, and business coaching for friends while my baby was young, and I had sharpened my skills.

What intrigued me in my work at Brass Tacks was that while I was striving to provide culturally affirming financial services, it was often not enough to make real change in people's habits. The tools on their own aren't enough. Folks still resist and avoid their money matters. People get regressive around their finances. My Scorpio rising wanted to know why. All this wondering and prying, combined with the spiritual reawak-ening I was experiencing through my divorce and eviction process, became a catalyst for my next business: Money Witch. That was 2013 and I've never looked back.

As Money Witch grew, and I engaged in intimate conversations with more and more people through my intuitive financial coaching practice, I saw how much pain was lying under the surface of my clients' relationships to money. Healing our finances is not just about changing our material circumstances; it gets to the heart of our core issues and what's hardest for us about being human. Seeing the potential for healing within each person's finances became the ethos that has guided my business for the last decade. Healing means movement of energy. When we move energy, we flush out stagnation. To do it intentionally, and especially magically, means we take control of the direction in which that shift and change happens. We intentionally strive for a shift that will answer our prayers.

Healing is an attempt to put broken pieces back together and to dissolve layers of debris that block us from operating as our highest selves. We address not only the places where we have been injured but also the places where our brokenness has allowed us to injure others. When we heal, we are addressing a wound or a trauma. While *trauma* is a word that gets associated with horrific events, all it actually means is that our nervous system experienced a situation as overwhelming and impossible to digest. We have to be conscious of the pace and dose of our healing because we don't want to reactivate that experience of nervous system overwhelm. The blocks we battle in our financial life indicate the debris of things we may not have been ready to process and digest when they occurred, as well as the coping strategies we developed over time to manage our traumas. A process of healing can activate in many different ways. Sometimes we have to be dragged kicking and screaming—confronted by what we can't seem to have in our lives, such as a romantic partnership, a satisfying sex life, or financial or career success. Sometimes there is a more gentle invitation to heal: Issues that you've been putting off for years start peeking their heads up, and synchronistic clues start calling you in. These invitations, however subtle or unsubtle they may be, push us to humble ourselves and release resistance to beginning the process of healing.

My own call to heal came around the time my child turned two. I really could viscerally feel a separation, returning to myself as an individual and not an enmeshed family unit. Pregnancy and birth were so incredibly transformative for me that when I was returning to my individuality, I had to integrate those experiences and meet myself as the new person I had become. I knew I was stronger than I had previously imagined. I was not as broken as I had always feared I was. I felt powerful, and I felt electric. My rising desire to embrace my personal power as well as my need for independence outside of our little nuclear family began creating conflict and then fissure in my marriage. I started reconnecting to the emotional and spiritual world with a depth and intensity I hadn't felt for a decade. I strengthened my friendships with people around me who were also experimenting with tarot, crystals, herbs, sacred sound, energy, sex magic, and psychic connections. I found the word *witch* for myself. I called a gathering with four other mystical Jewish friends to discuss what it would look like for us to practice together. This constellation became a coven. Our work together overflowed into community celebration and ritual making. It was the beginning of, or really a returning to, religious leadership and priestessing. I started drifting further away from my devout atheist partner, and what had previously been a quirky mismatch in our marriage became an impassable incompatibility. We were unable to relate spiritually. The shared political principles that had held our mutual value system together started splintering. My best friend says this is when I went from anarchist power wife to hot hippie mama. She's not wrong.

Every ounce of healing and change I have struggled to achieve, and every tool I have acquired on my meandering path, led me to become a vessel for both the spiritual practice and the business—Money Witch—that I have today.

WHY HEAL
YOUR FINANCES?

Transforming our relationship to money is possible and it is necessary. It will change our lives and empower our families and communities. Putting focus on healing yourself is deeply valuable to the community. We have so much more to give, from a more holistic place, when we prioritize self-awareness and self-development.

I am writing this book in the midst of a pandemic, a racialized uprising, a presidential election, and a devastating fire season. The intentional obscuring of large-scale, centuries-old systems of oppression is crumbling. Student loans, lack of accessible housing, and climate disaster are dissolving the facade of the "American dream" for even those privileged tiers who were ever allowed to invest in it in the first place. We are dealing with some major long-game, big-picture shit. Somehow in the midst of all this, we have to pay our bills, #hustleharder, #dowhatwelove, and not lose our damn minds. There is an urgency to our healing. We don't have time to be unaware, disorganized, or self-sabotaging. We need us to show up resourced to meet the moment.

Your path of transformation, your healing road, is up to you. It needs to be paved with your own financial values and priorities. The process of defining your path and how you travel down it is yours. A little guidance and a few tools never hurt, so I will be here to cheer you on with spiritual, emotional, and logistical support along the way. Even the fiercest of divas needs a support team. Most of us don't get the help that we need because we're too busy being strong and in service of others. Let this book hold space for you to figure out your next moves toward healing. Healing around money is special because you are unlocking the resources that feed and nourish you in everything else that you do. Having the funds to pay your bills, take care of yourself physically and mentally, contribute to the material support of your loved ones, and make it through an emergency makes your entire life more manageable. I care about you getting to have this, and I am here to share the language, the tools, and the lessons that I have gathered along my own healing path.

Most financial information does not feel accessible or appealing. I'm writing this book because I don't see myself reflected in a lot of financial education. I'm not a rule follower. I've had my car impounded (multiple times), I've been in credit card debt, I've been dependent on partners for money and felt controlled and like I'd never be empowered. I've been on food stamps and WIC and Medicare. I've lived in collective houses. I've held on to rent control for my dear life. I've been handed things and fumbled them, had opportunities and blown them. I've dropped out of college, I've been suspended from school, and my kid has too. My finances aren't perfect. But I have put in work on every front, invested in my own financial independence, and made movement. I'm not where I want to be either, and I keep working at it all the time. I heard someone say thirdhand about me, "The Money Witch? I heard she's not even rich." But y'all . . . that's the point!

I respect you as an individual, and I am not going to tell you that there is one path to healing or managing your finances. I am here to plant seeds and hold space for you to spend some time shining a light on the place where your psyche meets money. There is space for you to bring the prismatic reality of who you are and how you relate to money, formed through the combination of your experiences and the experiences of your ancestors, to meet this process. You are, in the words of one of my favorite rabbis, Reb Zalman, of blessed memory, a uniquely holographic particle of G-d. Your being and your experience are completely extraordinary and can never be replicated.

This is not a law of attraction book, although we will get woo and talk about the impact of your energy on your finances. I'm not going to shame you for not being a positive enough thinker and not inviting enough abundance into your life. We're not going to spiritually bypass the systemic issues that deeply impact people's finances. This book does not override systemic and intentional financial oppression, nor should you ever be pressured into taking responsibility for the impact of systemic oppression on your finances. This book focuses on what you do have control over: your internal experience and the ways you participate in disempowering yourself. Self-sabotage means we do the work of our oppressors for them. Stop participating in cultivating crisis for yourself. Start cultivating a self-loving relationship with money, success, ease, and being resourced. I believe that we can each respond to the call to step into greater maturity in our financial lives, and that we can learn how without shutting down due to overwhelm. Moving your mindset will change your relationship to practical things like taxes, budgeting, and your credit score. You deserve to feel more empowered and more connected.

Whichever way you got to this book, I see you showing up for yourself to heal. I see you, I am proud of you, and I offer you my love and admiration. Healing work, and especially shadow work—facing the parts of your subconscious that you've been ignoring and repressing—is no easy task. But you're making it happen for yourself, and that is so, so beautiful.

THE THREE ANGLES OF HEALING

To have the biggest impact and the most power in creating a healing shift, you'll need to address your issues through all three angles of healing:

Practical/Logistical

This is putting your feet on the ground to manifest your desires. The blessing unfolds through your actions. This angle includes things like getting that budget together, learning how to plan for your taxes, working toward paying down your debt, asking for a raise, or charging higher prices for your services. You can pray all day, figure out why you are the way you are, but if you don't get that tush in action, things aren't going to actualize on a material plane.

Spiritual/Emotional

This angle involves taking a good hard look in the mirror and asking yourself, "Why am I like this??" Seriously though, self-awareness is absolutely key to any kind of change and growth. This means unearthing the impact of the experiences and relationships that have formed you and your habits and patterns of behavior. When I say spiritual, I mean the path of your specific individual spirit on this Earth. This angle is all about cracking the code on *you*, your path, your current and historical ways of being, and where you need to be headed. Examples of tools that can assist you in this work are therapy, mindfulness and meditation, journaling, personality tests, astrology, and practices designed to help you access your subconscious, such as tarot and dream analysis.

Magical/Energetic

Magic means taking responsibility for yourself as an energetic entity. You have an energetic field; you are an energetic force, as is every organic entity in the Multiverse. When you own this fact, and engage with your energy responsibly and mindfully, you have the power to influence the energetic sphere around you and the energy of others as well. In magic, we acknowledge and honor the energetic power of every being and can ask them to mindfully ally with us in achieving our goals. This means calling on stones, plants, planets, elements, ancestors, archetypes, birds and other animals to align with us in our healing. This angle is about owning that you in combination with elemental forces and other energetic bodies have the power to create miracles.

You don't have to be a perfect witch, or even a witch at all, to activate healing magic. We're going to add some super simple rituals, affirmations, and manifestation exercises to every chapter so that you can put your magic, your particular sparkle, behind your work to heal your finances.

SEVEN STEPS TO A MORE MAGICAL RELATIONSHIP WITH MONEY

We are going to spend the rest of our time together journeying through my seven-step system to heal your finances. Every healing journey needs an entry point, and this book is designed to help you travel deeply into the spiritual/emotional angle of healing. The following chapters are organized to walk you through the process step by step, and since all three angles of healing are essential to creating a holistic shift, each section will include practical and magical exercises to ground your emotional work.

These steps set out a very clear healing path, and you can apply them to other areas of your life that may need healing in the future, any place you want to shift but are confronting wounding. But we're here to talk money! The seven steps are a modern babe's hero's journey to financial wellness.

The journey begins by developing self-awareness in order to find your current location and takes you to the final destination of achieving your goals. The steps along the way are filled with deep self-exploration, connecting the dots, and truth telling. We are going to honor your financial legacy, who you have been and how you got to be that way. We will thank your habits and coping mechanisms for serving to protect and comfort you when you needed them, and we will work to release what is no longer serving you, creating spaciousness in your psyche to develop a new relationship to money.

A lot of scary things may surface for you on your journey of healing your finances: shame, embarrassment, low self-esteem, guilt, self-imposed suffering and struggle, fear of yourself and of wealth, the impact of mental health struggles, ancestral trauma. We will honor and hold them all with respect and care, loving all of who we are. Rather than disowning these parts of ourselves, we will tend to them, ask them what they need, and provide skilled care so that we can liberate ourselves from their impact in our daily financial lives. Most important, we will be present with ourselves in the moment, and honestly reflect on our past, in order to stay future-focused. We can level up! And look amazing while doing it.

Some say, "Your net worth begins with your self-worth" or "Your bank account balance will never exceed your self-image." I don't think you have to be completely healed to get a fat check or a big bank account. I don't think you have to be completely healed to deserve love or be successful in a relationship either. But I do think that you owe it to yourself to get on and stay on the path to healing. And I definitely think when you clear some healing hurdles, your relationship with money will feel better, more lush and abundant, more calm and in control. Life is too short to fuck around wounded and unaware. So let's get that healing and let's get that money.

HOW TO
USE THIS BOOK

Each chapter in this book walks you through one of the Seven Steps to a More Magical Relationship with Money, containing advice and exercises to support your financial healing work. This book can support you in many different ways. If you read the book all the way through from front to back, you'll absorb a system you can use to heal your finances and, honestly, most anything else in your life as well. If you pick up this book periodically and flip through to find a paragraph of interest, there are plenty of standalone gems for you to discover, explore, and implement in your life. You can also use the ancient practice of bibliomancy, using books as a tool of divination. To receive a magical message about your financial healing journey, hold this book while asking a question, then close your eyes, open to a page, and put your finger on a paragraph. Spirit has brought you here!

You'll also find the following elements to help you on your journey:

MONEY MAGIC ALLIES: Each chapter opens with recommended allies for your journey, including astrological inspiration, crystals to get you vibrating higher, a tiny tarot reading, and a cup of tea made of herbs who've got your back. These friends will help you embody the energy of the chapter.

Completely optional extra-credit witch points for setting up a temporary altar with the recommended tarot cards and stones, while sipping on the tea and answering your journal questions for that chapter. Light a candle and vibe with yourself in the ultimate act of money magic self-care.

JOURNAL PROMPTS: Short writing prompts to inspire reflection and revelation. Taking time to respond to the information in the book will support you in fully digesting the thoughts, feelings, and reactions that are activated as you read.

If writing hurts your body or feels frustrating or not a good way to express your thoughts, then you could also voice-record a response, draw or paint a picture, or just take a minute or two to meditate on each prompt.

AFFIRMATIONS: Empowering declarations to remind yourself of your worth and potential. Affirmations are little bursts of aligned energy that you can use to propel yourself along your journey. Affirmations support and cheer us on to keep us headed toward our intention. Read them out loud or in your head to create powerful new habits of mind. Repeat regularly for a mindset makeover!

MINDFULNESS MOMENTS: Short contemplations to help you find calm, groundedness, and clarity on your path to healing. These are designed to help you check in with the wisdom of your body and tap into the experience your subconscious mind is having as you explore, activate, and heal. Try reading one out loud into a voice recorder and playing it back to enjoy a guided meditation experience.

HEAL YOUR FINANCES HOMEWORK: Practical opportunities for you to exercise your financial literacy muscle and build new habits.

RITUALS: Each chapter concludes with a ritual to help you activate the magic and close the container of what you just read and engaged with.

I believe in you and know you are completely capable of this transformative work. Here are a few last thoughts to keep you on path as we get started on this journey:

What If I'm Not Witchy Enough?

Not everything in this book is applicable to everybody, so if you don't feel acquainted with a certain spiritual practice, or you need more information, don't sweat it or feel alienated. This book has something for everyone, whether you're a total magical beginner or an experienced spiritual practitioner.

If something is exciting to you, but you don't know how it works, such as tarot cards, take this as a synchronistic invitation to do some research, learn more, and then come back to engage with those tools. They are for you too, if you want them to be.

The Magical Oracle of the Internet

The world of the internet has so many treasures and teachers for you, so just start out by entering a query in your search bar:

- How to use tarot cards
- How to look at my shadow self
- How to make a spiritual offering

Also

- How do I open a Roth IRA
- How do I apply for a car loan
- How do I start a side hustle
- How do reparations work

Remember that people on the internet, such as social media, are real, and have lives and finite time and energy resources. So make sure you start your journey with some solo research before you ask questions. Once you've got some of your basic questions answered, engage with teachers in right relationship, which means thinking about what you are offering in return for what you are asking, and respecting the boundaries and limitations they set out. Some teachers and practitioners offer entry-level guidance and some do not. Some folks respond to DMs, emails, and comments and some do not. Always look to see if your desired educator has a paid offering that corresponds to the knowledge you are seeking, or if they list a way to tip them, before expecting your curiosities to be answered for free. There are no dumb questions, but there are entitled ones.

Engage!

While you're reading this book, make it yours. Underline or highlight the passages that excite or scare you; write your responses in the margins. Yell your responses out loud. Argue with me.

Decorate a new notebook to make some space to work on the journal prompts.

Practice Self-Care

Be aware of your needs as they arise. Get up and stretch when you tense up. Take a walk and a break if something in the book is bringing up responses you need to sit with longer. Nurture yourself with a cozy blanket and some tea while reading. Talk it out with a friend. Hydrate. Notice when you need soothing, and give it to yourself.

STEP

1

Own Your Capacity for Change, or Why You're Not the Worst Person in the World

---

*Overcome shame and guilt to fulfill
your potential to heal.*

MONEY MAGIC ALLIES

Astrological Role Model

Scorpio: Scorpio knows that in order to find your fullest power, you have to be willing to burn down the whole damn thing to find a tiny seed of authentic, aligned truth and rebuild from there. Scorpio knows that sometimes you are the phoenix and sometimes you are the puddle of ashes, but it is all an offering on the altar of your deepest purpose and sovereignty. Letting go of outdated ways of being can be scary, but when you rebuild in alignment with your highest self, life will feel so much more joyful and easeful. Give yourself the gift of an update.

Crystal Friends

Amazonite: Amazonite attracts money luck and ensures success when taking a chance. It's traditionally used by gamblers; in this case, you're betting on yourself. This bluish-green stone wards off negative influences, pessimism, fatigue, the residue of trauma, blockages within the nervous system, and anything else that might deplete your energy and prevent you from being able to embrace opportunities. Clearing off this psychic debris will heighten your receptivity to money, luck, and overall success.

Chrysoprase: Chrysoprase taps you into the divine purpose of your life, the wisdom that you are holy and have a uniquely sacred path to walk on Earth. You hold all knowledge about this path inside of you. This green apple–colored stone will assist you in acknowledging and accessing this information, as well as the courage you need to implement it in your life.

Tiny Tarot Reading

Death and The Empress: This power pair represents the entire experience of spiritual rebirth: death, the void, and the creation of new life. Being born anew into infinite abundance means suffering the pain of letting go of old versions of yourself and the ego death that goes with it. It also means spending time gestating in the void—the place where there is no answer yet, where nothingness holds hands with infinite potential, getting broken down by the cosmic compost pile. There is no need to resist change; your past experiences are a blessing and have been your teachers. You have to let go because you are ready to level up. Own your new level by naming it, claiming it, truly releasing that which no longer serves you, and stepping into the immeasurable abundance of the Multiverse.

Cup of Tea

Cinnamon, ginger, and dandelion root will flush stagnation from the body and introduce movement and flow.

used to think of this step as a pre-step, something to check in about before the real work begins. My actual bad. This step contains some of the heavy lifting of this whole process. For some of you, this step may feel like an easy one. Yup, got it, I can change, that's why we're here, on to the next step. For others, as soon as you read the title of the chapter, your heart may have beat a little faster. You may have disassociated a little bit. So let's check in: Are we breathing?

If you're in the first group, just ride along with us for a bit while we regulate. If you're in the second group, you may be flooded with a montage of all the things you wish were different about you and your life but aren't. Your brain may be overrun with tiny critical voices reminding you of past failed attempts at change. Remember when you were going to go to the gym, or meal prep, or budget? You might be ruminating on other people's stories about you—the projections that your parents, partners, and authority figures have heaped on you since your inception. These stories may be that you're not good with money, you're spoiled, irresponsible, you never finish anything. They may be just the opposite—that you're the savior of the family, the great hope, generations of unfulfilled dreams pinned on your education, your career, and your financial success. You may have had to take responsibility for meeting the material needs of yourself, your siblings, your parents, or a child at an early age. You may feel like you can never change, or it might not feel safe to you to take the risks necessary to change. Maybe you just feel hopeless, that you're stuck in a situation or a set of habits that you cannot fathom being any different.

You're wrong. Not only are you capable of transformational change, but you've already demonstrated it in your life and you are engaged in it right now. Let's honor all the ways we have evolved in our lifetimes, praise every stretch out of our comfort zones, from the tiniest flutter of hope to the biggest boss moves. Showing up for yourself, entering the discomfort zone of transition and change, and expanding your belief of what is possible for you is the work of revolution. This work will heal you on a cellular level. It will expand to send healing to your relationships, your family, your communities, and our larger societal framework. This is both the work of becoming sovereign (stepping into full authority and power in your own life) and the work of healthful, resourced interdependency. This is the work.

Since you're reading a magical self-help book (and I'm writing one), I'm going to go out on a limb and say we're a pretty hopeful bunch. We probably believe that people can change. Whether we like it or not, we're regularly reminded that change is the only constant. We may have even seen dramatic examples of successful change in our lifetime—parents getting sober, romantic partnerships mending after a violation of trust, that time we went vegan. Despite all the evidence and predilection, a belief deep inside stubbornly says, *Other people can change but I can't.*

In step 1, we're going to accept ourselves as deeply human and deeply worthy in order to work through shame, guilt, and other societally imposed junk that holds us back from our true power. Stop mistreating yourself and beating yourself up. Thinking you're the worst person in the world is just as flawed as thinking you're the best. We are all human, we are all flawed, we are all special, and we all have the potential to heal.

The goal of this step is to create a solid foundation for change so that we can begin the work of building our dream finances. You can bring positive change to your financial life. I promise you that both your relationship to money and your material reality can be different.

This change you are embarking on is not because something is wrong with you. You're not changing for anyone else, although you may see benefit to your relationships with your family, your partners, and your community. You are changing to bring yourself more in alignment with yourself. This is a sacred act—to return to who you know you are, to return to your highest self. This change is for you. Bringing your behavior into alignment with your path, your power, and your purpose is called integrity.

YOU DESERVE
A PROCESS

"We are worthy enough to be restored." I came across this quote memorializing the loss of Elandria Williams, a solidarity economy activist and Unitarian Universalist church leader, whose blessed soul passed to the other side of the veil in 2020. These synchronistic words came to me right when I needed them and bolstered me up in a time where I was struggling with my own self-worth. It can be hard to believe that we deserve the space to heal, and hard to take enough responsibility to actually do it. But it is evidenced by our very existence that we deserve the chance to try, and that the Universe supports our efforts at redemption.

We are also worthy of a process for transformation. The world we are collectively creating is built from the micro to the macro. This means if we want our societal systems to let go of injurious patterns, we must allow ourselves the same experience of transformation. How we relate to our own sphere of life radiates out to how we show up in community, and how our communities are constructed radiates out to build culture and social structures. Let's make space for change and growth in all these places by honoring our human right to the process of healing. As my racial healing and equity coach, MeLisa Moore, has taught me, there is something bigger for us than just a reduction of harm.

A change always involves a process, and a process can be messy as hell. We might be afraid that a change will be like a fissure, breaking apart the systems of survival that we have carefully constructed. The ways we survive in this world can feel tenuous, and we hold them tightly together through controlling behavior and emotions. A change can mean being out of control for a little while. A change means spending some time in the void, a place of infinite potential but apparent nothingness. All these experiences can be scary, confusing, and less than appealing. Spending time in the process of growth forces you to cultivate very important, precious, and vulnerable tools: hope, faith, and equanimity. You deserve this process and these tools.

MINDFULNESS MOMENT

Infinite Power

What if we are infinitely powerful?

Sit comfortably in a chair or on the floor, and focus your energy on the place where your body touches the ground. As you breathe in, visualize Earth energy drawing up into your body to support and stabilize you. You are a part of this Earth.

Move your focus up to your heart center, and give yourself some love. Imagine yourself connected to a web of powerful, grounded, loving energy. The most powerful and unconditional love you can imagine is pouring through your body, cleansing your heart and radiating out effortlessly to touch others. Breathe, and imagine yourself as a conduit for this deeply healing energy. Feel how you are changed by receiving and giving this powerful substance. Allow it to pour into every limb and every cell of your body.

Your human existence is infinitely powerful and full of transformational capacity. Be changed by this love; allow it to change you and open your heart to more evolution. Allow this cleansing energy to flow through you and then down through the place you grounded at the start of the meditation. Allow the self-doubt, self-hatred, and fear that cleared from your heart to pour back down to the Earth. Don't worry about harming the Earth with your heavy debris; it is ready to be neutralized and regenerated in an energetic compost process.

Come back to your body and back to the present.

Change almost always costs us something. We might have to shift our idea of ourselves, who and what we think we are. We might have to admit that our old way of doing something wasn't great after all. Evolution can be hard when we're overly invested in our identity or personality. What are you willing to sacrifice in order to step more deeply into a place of true empowerment? So much of "who we are" is defined by our coping mechanisms, ways of being that we developed to deal with circumstances that didn't truly support us. It's scary to let go of old ways of being, particularly if we have invested time, energy, or lip service to them being "good" or "right" ways to be. The most terrifying part can be that in letting go of things, we know that we are changing and moving toward something, but we often don't know what is awaiting us, and what it will look like, feel like, or be like.

The stakes of allowing ourselves this process are nothing less than the salvation of our humanity. Reclaiming our humanity means understanding our desires, taking the needs of our body and our material life seriously, and believing we are deserving. There's nothing wrong with us, our needs, and the journey we take toward meeting them.

As we begin this healing path, we might feel hard feelings—shame, embarrassment, pridefulness, scarcity, fear. These feelings hold us hostage, trying to convince us that we'll never make it through. They tell us that the messiness we have to go through in order to heal is a bad look, that it makes us ugly and unlovable. Ultimately, we fear we don't deserve the space to have a human process—which, if we're going to get into it, means we fear we don't deserve to exist.

There've been several times in my life where I could barely believe how incredibly broken down everything in my life had become. Divorcing, evicted with a three-year-old, and poorer than I'd ever been. Struggling to deal with emotional and financial abuse, my kid suspended from school, and my car needing a $10,000 repair (thank Goddess for insurance). Devastatingly heartbroken, ill, suicidal, and on a work deadline. Really, actually! Each one of these periods of my life broke me down and built me back up. I was never the same afterward, but in so many ways I was better. There is an initiation that is available to you in times of unavoidable change, an invitation to greater spiritual knowing, a welcoming to become a wiser, more humble, and more empathetic person. To become more deeply human.

AFFIRMATION

I am changing my feelings and habits around money.

Having to be broken down, admit wrongdoing, and lay down our defenses is part of the transformation process. It's scary to let go, but you deserve something better. Even when things aren't good for us, we can be attached to them. We can be attached to parts of our personalities, and even feel loyalty toward the self-harming ones. We may feel especially protective of these parts of ourselves. Our whole self, including our injured, feral parts, deserve this process too; they deserve to heal and mature.

JOURNAL PROMPT
Ch-ch-ch-changes

What positive examples of change have you witnessed in your life, either in yourself or others? What is one way you are more in integrity with yourself today than you were one year ago?

SHAME AS A TOOL OF SOCIAL CONTROL

We're going to get real pretty fast here: If you can't get past this step, you're wrestling with shame. Shame is a deep wound, and indicates our discomfort at even existing. It forms when we witness ourselves and the things that are important to us being threatened and devalued. Shame carves itself into us in childhood and is reinforced by social norms reflected in media, school, workplace, and relationships. Shame is a symptom and side effect of kyriarchal culture. Kyriarchy is an incredibly useful term we'll all wish we knew sooner; it names the overarching structure of societal power obsessed with domination and oppression. Kyriarchy is what we mean when we say "settler-colonial capitalist white supremacist ableist cis hetero patriarchy." Except we get to say just one word, and that's nice. Kyriarchy, which was coined in 1992 by Professor Elisabeth Schüssler Fiorenza, describes the social system that creates the

AFFIRMATION

I have agency in this experience of change.

circumstances described by the theory of intersectionality, an experience of condition named by professor and lawyer Kimberlé Crenshaw in 1989. This "matrix of domination" (named by Patricia Hill Collins in 1990 in her book *Black Feminist Thought*) is both externally imposed and self-sustained by internalized oppression. Shame is internalized oppression. Please don't lose your precious life force to shame.

Money and shame get linked in our psyches so quickly and so early that it can be hard to pull them apart. We feel shame because we have too little or too much. We take on the belief that our lack of access to the resources that we need, materially or emotionally, is directly connected to our lack of worthiness.

Shame is related to a family of feelings that show up regularly on the money journey. Let's get to know them here, so that we can be on the same page when we're referencing them:

GUILT is the feeling that you've done something wrong. This is a feeling of belief or recognition that an action you've taken has had a negative impact on another person or yourself. Guilt may sometimes be an indicator that you are weighing your actions against an external measure of judgment rather than your own.

SHAME is the feeling that you are wrong, that something is inherently wrong with you, or that you are undeserving, inadequate, or inferior.

INTEGRITY is meeting the standard of your personal measure of judgment. Integrity is about weighing your own actions against your own values and priorities and assessing whether they are in alignment or not. When you act without integrity, you damage your self-image and your self-esteem.

HUMILITY is standing in honesty and radical acceptance of who and where you are. It means acknowledging your humanity, apologizing when you make mistakes, engaging in lifelong inner transformation, and simultaneously recognizing both the preciousness and the relative smallness of your individual human life. Humility is a powerful antidote to shame culture.

I want to say clearly and with deep compassion: Shame is an absolute waste of time. It is not casual, and it is not easy, but it is absolutely necessary to do everything you can to drive the demon of shame out of your body and out of your life. What if we are not terrible at all? What if we are infinitely powerful? What eclipses our greatness? Let's believe in something greater for ourself: becoming more free, more happy, more embodied, more at peace, and more resourced, both materially and emotionally.

THE ONE PERSON YOU CAN NEVER LEAVE

Not taking care of our finances is a symptom of self-abandonment. Refusing to show up for our most basic needs of material survival is a symptom of self-neglect. We're taught to be able to identify tangible and explicit types of abuse, such as physical or verbal. Experiencing mistreatment through abandonment and neglect is even more common. If you are someone who has experienced abuse or mistreatment by others in your life, you're not alone. These experiences leave us much to heal, including the propensity to inflict similar harm on ourselves.

The ways we perpetuate neglect and abandonment in our relationship to ourself can be hard to identify. Behaviors of abandonment and neglect generally result from a deep lack of emotional and/or material resources. Just as our caretakers may have felt under-resourced for and overwhelmed by the job of providing for us, we can feel that same way about the assignment of providing for ourself. Notice any part of you that feels fatigued and underprepared for the task of self-care. Notice how and when that part of you subconsciously decides to neglect the duty of adequate care. Give this part of you so much compassion, but also a request for accountability. Your journey to heal your finances requires that you participate fully and stay present with all parts of yourself—the neglected and the neglector—as you all heal and ease the internal conflict. Do not disown essential parts of yourself, including both the part that needs stability, security, and less struggle, and the part that is challenged by providing and managing those things. You need you.

MINDFULNESS MOMENT

The Shame Game

Shame manifests differently for each of us. I can personally feel its presence through a tingling sensation in my cheeks and a tightness in my forehead and throat. What physical sensations arise in your body to tell you that you feel shame?

As you even read or think about shame, this physical sensation may creep up. Take a moment to notice it.

THIS EARTH JOURNEY

Your primary spiritual purpose at this moment in time is to be exactly perfectly human. The news that we're made of stardust and lived a past life in Atlantis (I was right there with you) is thrilling, but babe, right now you are human on Earth in the twenty-first century. The point is not to glaze over this assignment and get back to being cosmic ASAP. For fourteen billion years, the particles that make up your body existed in this Universe, but not as you. They prayed to become you. Your ancestors prayed you into existence. Your soul was led to your exact body by angels who nurtured you into existence. So much miraculous labor went into making your human incarnation possible. You are a miracle! Your presence in the human story at this particular point in time-space is not an accident. You are filled with purpose; your human life is inextricably bound up with your spiritual purpose. This is to say, the seemingly mundane and often tedious tasks of figuring out how to be a human are not mundane at all. Being and becoming better at human life is all you have to do in this lifetime.

As animals, material survival is the basis of that work, and since here we are in late-stage global capitalism, when I say material survival, I mean money. It's not an accident for you to be born into these systems. You have something to contribute to making this exact moment better, or you wouldn't be here. Connecting to the human experience from a soul-centered place is a very powerful way of exploring life, but don't forget that physical survival is a big part of your soul's work in this incarnation. This work of healing your finances is not an aside; it is the work of healing everything in your life. You are here on this Earth to evolve, and to weave the unique thread of your journey into the tapestry of human existence. When you expand into success in all areas of your life, you contribute more deeply to the communal healing of your lineages and communities, as well as the entire human story.

It's important to note that just because money is spiritual doesn't mean we can talk about it or work on it without acknowledging systemic economic oppression. Talking about an issue as spiritual while trying to sidestep the "unresolved emotional issues, psychological wounds, and unfinished developmental tasks" of either ourselves as individuals or the societies we live in is called spiritual bypassing, as phrased by John Welwood, a Buddhist teacher and psychotherapist who introduced the term in the early 1980s. We can't spiritual our way out of being human or being in relationship with the human experience. Being spiritual is inherently human and must hold the truth of humanity. The ways that spiritual bypassing shows up in conversations around manifestation, the law of attraction, and money magic are harmful, violent, and wounded. No manifestation process should pressure you to ignore the impact of marginalization or the reality that our money story has massive chapters in it, including the current one, that are based on the exploitation of human life and labor (especially Black and Indigenous lives) and the unsustainable extraction of the Earth's resources (due to the violent suppression of Indigenous stewardship). No conversation about financial healing can be based on gaslighting that this is not even happening.

It can be confusing and frustrating to try to hold both the spiritual purpose of life and a pervasive experience of structural inequalities. The friction between these truths is just one example of the major paradoxes of being human. Sitting with paradox is the realest of human experiences. So the good part is, as we've talked about in this chapter, being human is all we have to do in this life. These double binds push us to find creative solutions, be genius, and discover the unique nuances of our own truth. They also give us an opportunity to do something deeply human: acknowledge we are a part of a much larger story, accept the things we cannot change, and fight like hell to change what we can, starting with ourselves.

So much of how we got where we are financially has been out of our control. The human form we take has a spiritual purpose, but it also has a randomness to it that is entirely unfair. While we are in the process of facing the particular set of challenges we have been dealt, we are going to experience anger. Give this anger some space. Ask your anger what it needs. Making space for the emotion will allow it to feel seen and heard, which is what we all need. Try to find some safe space to express anger. Making conscious space to metabolize anger means allowing yourself to feel it as fully as you can and allowing it to move through and out of your body through such actions as artistic expression, screaming in the car, punching a pillow, ripping paper, or exercise so that it doesn't live repressed as your shadow self. What practices do you have in your life for metabolizing anger?

As you dig deeper into your money story, it is normal for anger, rage, and grief to surface. Think of these feelings as bubbles of stored energy that will naturally come to the surface when the firmament of your money trauma is being broken down. Your job is to make space for them to be released rather than re-cementing them in the new structure you are building for yourself. The process of living within kyriarchy means that within our money story there are places where we have been or are being mistreated, where we have or are experiencing abuse, and where we ongoingly compromise our values in order to survive. Allow yourself space to notice, feel, and express your anger about systemic financial oppression so that it doesn't manifest as self-harming behavior. For example, a lot of people avoid filing their taxes on time because they feel (justifiably) angry at the ways their government is spending their money. But in reality, all this does is make you pay more money to that very same government in interest and penalties, cause stress in your own life, and sometimes even cause you to miss out on a refund if you wait too long to file.

Acknowledging these experiences and validating the anger that right-fully accompanies them will go a long way in giving you the space to reconcile with money. You're not angry at money; you're angry at systemic oppression, at your family, at financial abuse and manipulation you have experienced. Being angry at money will keep you stuck in the same place you've been in, because it locks you in an adversarial relationship. If you can't start to let go of your anger with money, it is very challenging to build a loving relationship with it. If you can't let go of your anger at yourself for some of the ways you may have acted with your finances in the past, it is very challenging to build a loving relationship with money. A self-loving relationship with money is our goal, and you deserve to get there. Your resistance energy is sacred and deeply needed by the human collective; please don't waste it on your finances.

JOURNAL PROMPT

Get Mad

What makes you feel angry about your finances? How do you know when you are feeling angry? How do you make space in your life to express anger healthfully? Do you give yourself permission to feel and express anger even when it's not societally affirmed?

THE CHALLENGE IS WHAT CHANGES YOU

It may have seemed impossible to change your finances in the past. It may have been impossible to imagine ever feeling different about money, ever caring enough about it to prioritize the effort, or ever seeing a tangible positive shift in your financial life. You may have felt that money is dirty and corrupting. You might still feel like that. That's OK. You may feel that the challenge of separating the organization of your personal finances under a capitalist system from your disgust toward capitalism is impossible. You may feel like having your finances under your own control is such a Sisyphean task that it's hard to even relate to the idea. It might feel like this isn't for you. I guarantee you that this is for you. This book is for you, these ideas are for you, comprehension and literacy and control are for you. Intentionality and comfort are for you. Agency and sovereignty are for you. Financial health is integral to your healing—all of it. Focusing on your means and methods of survival is not an immoral or unspiritual chore. You deserve to be met with financial tools that are relevant.

In order for a tool to be relevant, it has to hold the political, the spiritual, the emotional, the visionary, and the ancient. No wonder you may not have found the tools that would help you get a grasp on your finances! No wonder you feel like financial tools and success belong to someone else, and aren't meant for you. Feeling disconnected, overwhelmed, and disempowered as a result of that is very sane and very normal.

The responsibility of change is a big deal. To live in a better world, we have to become better. To have better finances, we have to stand in our power to make them better. This is a wake-up call to be in greater integrity and alignment with your power and divine purpose. It's hard to face the places where we're not quite there yet. It's normal to be afraid of responsibility. It's also normal to view change as threatening. But these attitudes disempower you and deny your inherent capacity and qualifications to rock your one precious life.

I want to make space to acknowledge that if you haven't been in control of major changes in your life, and if your experiences have demonstrated to you that most major changes are bad, even considering the idea of change can cause shutdown. Change itself can feel traumatic, even if we are changing for the good. Center in your own agency this time. Where are the places that you are excited about making change, where you want to invite it and nurture it? You are an adult now. You have many more tools than you have had in prior times. Every day you become more capable. It may be helpful to pair this process with some nervous system–based trauma repair work, such as Somatic Experiencing or EMDR (Eye Movement Desensitization and Reprocessing). Also just give your nervous system some love during this process if you have a history of change being traumatic.

We know that both inner and outer change require us to let go of the branch we've been clinging to so we can leap (and move and heal) and grab on to the next one. In other words, change requires trust, and Lord knows a lot of us have trust issues. Change also requires faith—trust in something we cannot see. We may not have seen role models for a way of being that fully reflects who we want to be: stable without stagnation, powerful without grasping for power over others, successful on our own terms, valued without conforming to normative signposts of success. We may have played the game, done everything we were "supposed" to do, believing and internalizing the equation that says institutional power

+ hard work = success and stability. Or we may have resisted "success" altogether, basically believing that it wasn't for us. But we all dream of success, and I think we can use faith to keep working toward a world in which we are allowed to claim our success without assimilation and conformity to colonial, white supremacist, patriarchal, hierarchical systems. This means letting go of the parts of ourselves that are invested in those systems, and those forms of success, to claim our own power and our own lane. It means divesting from competition and hierarchy. It also means staying persistent in your right to define success for yourself and engage in an individual process of getting there. You are here to share your unique gifts formed by the combination of your soul (your long-term cosmic self) and your earthly circumstances (your upbringing and position in the world) with the larger human community. I personally believe success is achieved when your gift is received, valued, and reciprocated through recognition, and ideally money! Success is you being in right relationship with the larger human family.

HEAL YOUR FINANCES HOMEWORK

Make That Change

Take one step forward and experience healing! Identify one financial or administrative loose end from your past that you have felt ashamed of, and make a plan to clean it up.

This may be a debt you owe to a friend, a small past-due account lingering on your credit report, a defaulted account. Maybe you moved and haven't updated your driver's license or voter's registration. Maybe you've been meaning to get renter's insurance or make a living will.

Instead of feeling overwhelmed by the whole big behemoth of your finances, choose one bite-size project, make a clear and manageable plan, and implement the hell out of it.

RITUAL

Married to the Money

Use amulet magic to commit to your financial healing journey. An amulet is also known as a good luck charm and is meant to offer protection, support, and abundance to the wearer. This charm represents your dedication to inviting abundance into your life, like getting married to prosperity!

This particular amulet will serve as a talisman to protect and energize you on your financial healing journey. You will choose several small items and place them together in a small bag, bottle, tin, or locket. Almost any object can function as an amulet, so follow your intuition and don't be a perfectionist about it. The most important part of choosing elements is that they have special meaning for you. Commonly used items include gems or jewelry, coins, plant or animal parts, drawings or writing, and small statues, figurines, or dolls. My general recipe for amulet making includes a protective element, a supportive or grounding element, an element that encourages flow and vitality, and one item that binds everything together. Following this recipe, you might have a special bag filled with a lucky penny, a piece of black tourmaline, and some tulsi sewn shut with special thread or a walnut shell filled with gold leaf, dandelion root, and glitter sealed shut with wax. Just like a wedding ring, the magic is in your relationship to the item, so the amulet is brought to life by your prayer and engagement with it. The warmth of your body activates the amulet and absorbs its energy into your vibrational field. You can carry it in your pocket, wear it around your neck, pin it to the inside of your clothes, or place it above your bed.

Write a vow to yourself that outlines the commitments you are making, and celebrate your self-love. Pay attention to your financial health in times of stress and relaxation, in times of abundance and limitation, and commit to walking with abundance for as long as you both shall live.

STEP

2

Stop Being Polite and Start Getting Real

Ground in self-awareness through an accurate assessment of your behaviors, feelings, and opinions about money.

MONEY MAGIC ALLIES

Astrological Role Model

Aquarius: Aquarius knows that the first step in finding a genius solution to any problem is detached observation and data to understand the landscape of the big picture. While this detached energy can seem cold, what Aquarius really wants is for you to approach your information gathering as a scientist and not a judge. In that spirit, explore the world of your personal finances seeking only to understand what is currently true. Aquarius uses their data to bring radical social change and disrupt the current paradigm. Where do you want to be a revolutionary in your own life? Think about what revolutionary change you are excited about in your relationship with money. Gather data about your financial landscape in order to make positive change.

Crystal Friends

Fluorite: Fluorite is your friend for mental clarity, making good choices, and maximizing your intellectual capacity. An excellent stone for your desk or workspace, this green-to-purple-gradient stone increases powers of concentration and confidence in decision-making. Fluorite clears cloudiness and mental fog, and can be your friend in organizing and processing large amounts of information quickly to bring mental clarity and stability, even when things seem chaotic.

Amethyst: Amethyst brings you back to yourself. It gently blocks out distractions and compelling derailments that pull you off your path so that you calmly and naturally return. When you follow your path, you are walking in alignment with your best self, the highest, most actualized purpose of this human life, and in attunement with what Spirit has planned for you. Remember who you are; remember why you're here. One of amethyst's methods in guiding you toward clarity and discernment is to gift you self-awareness. This purple stone restores your focus on what's important, allowing you to make wiser decisions and release harmful influences and attachments.

Tiny Tarot Reading

The Hermit and The Hanging One: After truthful observation of the self comes the peace of acceptance. Understand that every part of your journey contributes to who you are and who you will become. There is no way to know where our path will lead; we can only work to plan a trustworthy next step. Stillness of the body, mind, and ego will allow you to find the most accurate inner compass—the one that directs you toward becoming a vessel for the divine light and gifts that are your birthright. Spend the time to fully be present with yourself and your truth before you act. Acknowledge all sides of yourself and get to know the parts of yourself that you have disowned and pushed to the margins. Those parts are also worthy and wise. Invest in time alone so that you can build trust with your own inner wisdom.

Cup of Tea

Tulsi rose will allow you to remain trusting and openhearted while processing stressful, anxiety-producing, or agitating information.

On our journey to a more magical relationship with money, this step represents our current location and starting point. In order to create an accurate map of how to get where you want to go, you've got to fully identify your current location. This means seeing yourself: who you are in the current moment, how you behave, and what environment you inhabit. It also means taking a look at which parts of your current environment are systemic or structural and out of your control, and which parts manifest from your behavior and vibration. Ultimately, this is just an exercise in self-awareness, which is the basis for any move toward change and growth. When you're looking to upgrade anything in your life, a self-awareness audit is always a foundational step!

Don't let your inner critic get too excited, because in order to get the most accurate read on your own behavior, you've got to drop the judgment. No one wants to expose their truths to a mean girl. We're here to be positive, create a winning team, and make changes, not be berated and belittled. I have seen some very compassionate people, people who even work in healing professions, get very mean with themselves about money. We want your inner self to feel open and comfortable in sharing their truthful opinions and feelings about money with us, and we want to have an accurate and neutral eye out to observe our behaviors without heaping on guilt, shame, and other self-abusive punishments. It might feel uncomfortable to strike a balance, but we're gonna breathe through it and cultivate gentleness without indulging in avoidance.

So much of Money Witch is built off of my own personal growth journey, my journey of observing myself and activating self-aware change. Taking hard looks at the babe in the mirror has been a daily practice for almost a decade now. This led me to a deepening practice of spirituality in its manifest forms. I started with weekly therapy, and gradually incorporated pulling a daily tarot card to reflect on, getting astrology readings, journaling, analyzing my dreams, joining a coven, and going to psychic school. All the most spiritually aware people I know, people you'd think had it all figured out already, put in time every day on their existential journey. There are so many different lenses through which to observe yourself, and so much reward from exploring all angles and vantage points to your life. Money is a lens we don't always incorporate on the journey to self-awareness, but it is a potent one that will liberate so much abundance in the rest of your life. Self-awareness can become a sanctuary, a place you experience grounding, and a launchpad to actualize your dreams.

In this step we're going to walk through several different exercises designed to help you look at yourself honestly and bring your financial landscape into focus. The goal of this step is to see clearly both the nuts and bolts of your finances and your attitudes and feelings about money.

MEET YOURSELF
WHERE YOU'RE AT

Since we're here to create that winning support team and get you where you need to go, let's get real practical for a moment about the best way to approach someone who needs help. In this case, the person who needs help is you. "Meet people where they're at" is a pretty commonly used phrase in the helping professions, such as social work, therapy, education, coaching, and medicine. Meeting yourself where you're at means taking a neutral but engaged look at what seems to be true and getting to know yourself for real. It means engaging with openness instead of heaping on expectation, disappointment, shame, or judgment of where you "should" be. I'm sure I'm not alone in having the experience of not being met where I was at, and having someone who was trying to "help" me make me feel worse, or even traumatized or unsafe. There's plenty of clueless, dangerous jerks out here dishing out "help," so there's absolutely no need to be that guy to ourselves.

Be honest with yourself about where you're at and be honest about what you don't know. You don't need to be ashamed of not already knowing how to do things better, you just have to be open to change. Finances are not necessarily intuitive, and not all of us had savvy role models. Not knowing how to do something is frustrating, but wanting to try something new is also a sign that you're growing. When we limit ourselves to areas in which we feel confident that we can already excel, we limit our growth and our wonder. The goal is not to become a perfect person or fit a mold of a "fiscally responsible" person; the goal is to be more you, to be so you that your wholeness spreads to every area of your life, including your finances. The goal is for you to feel like there's no area of your life that you need to hide from.

JOURNAL PROMPT
Who's the Boss?

When you think about how you "should" manage your finances more responsibly, who are you trying to please? Is it a parent, a partner, a family member, the bank, the patriarchy, the IRS?

ASSESSING YOUR FINANCIAL LANDSCAPE

Now that you've got your compassionate observer activated, it's time to take a deep look at what's going on in your money life. There are two parts to this assessment work. One is looking at the outer landscape of your financial reality, the practical landscape in which you exist. This includes looking at your income, your spending, your assets, your potential for earning, what debt you have, what your retirement savings and goals are—all that fun stuff. I want you to have a very clear grasp of what you're navigating on a practical and material level as we work through the steps. But don't worry, we won't be spending a lot of time there, as our primary concern through this book is the emotional world that's connected to the outer landscape. So please don't be a perfectionist about it. If doing the most is going to have you doing nothing at all, then drop it and move on to the assessment of your inner landscape. Don't put the book down!

The second part is assessing your inner landscape. This includes habits, feelings, behaviors, and history. Be gentle with yourself during this exploration, as this can be activating or triggering work, just like any kind of emotional excavation. You may have looked at these parts of yourself dozens of times before in therapy, workshops, tarot readings, or your journal, or this may be your first time really thinking about your financial self. Self-awareness involves noticing parts of yourself that are louder and more dramatic, as well as getting silent and making space and time to listen to your quieter ways of communicating.

YOUR OUTER LANDSCAPE: TAKING INVENTORY OF YOUR STORY

OK, let's take a look at that practical outer landscape first. This is the most numbers-y thing we're going to do in the whole book, so remember to breathe and let's just knock it out. Make a cup of tea, light a candle, and get out your notebook or open a spreadsheet. You're going to need your computer or phone. And, perhaps most challenging of all, you're going to need all your damn passwords to all your freaking accounts. Another deep breath.

So many of us avoid handling our financial business because we hate dealing with bureaucracy (and by hate, I mean it activates a spectrum of feelings that can range from annoyance to disempowerment to feeling actively unsafe). Try to validate these feelings for yourself and be ready for them. Engage practices that will counter the frustration, such as deep breathing, grounding exercises, taking a nervine tincture, lighting a scented candle you enjoy, or having a nice snack. Calm your nervous system down. And don't forget to call on your Money Magic Allies—that's what they're here for.

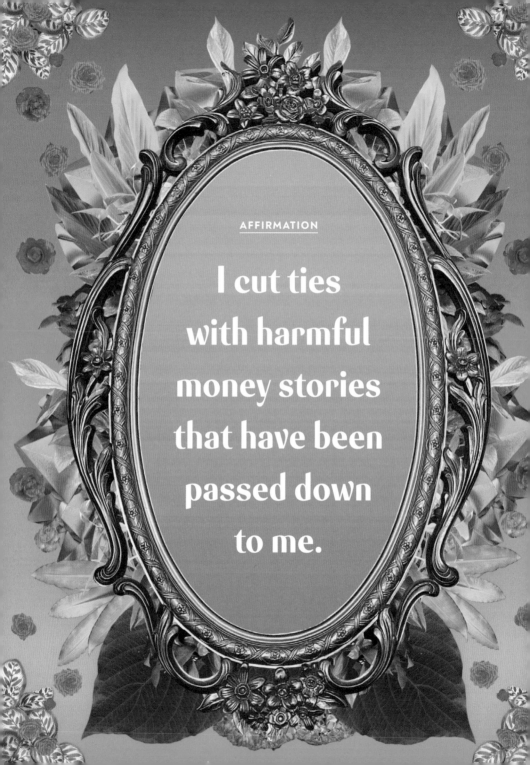

AFFIRMATION

I cut ties
with harmful
money stories
that have been
passed down
to me.

MINDFULNESS MOMENT

Just Passing Through

Take a moment to check in with what is happening inside of you as you think about looking at your finances. What are you feeling inside your body? Do you feel tight and contracted? Do you feel a tingle of nervous excitement? Do you feel grounded determination, do you feel disassociated and floaty, do you want to cry? Notice each sensation and hold it lightly, a very real piece of information, but one that is ultimately a cloud passing through your life. Every sensation and emotion you feel is a temporary visitor; treat it with curiosity, care, and grace.

When you've been avoiding looking at your finances for a long while, and you finally schedule a time to get down to it, it can feel insanely frustrating to be thwarted in your efforts and not be able to just get it accomplished. Don't set yourself up for disappointment with an all-or-nothing attitude. Instead, think of the long game. Show up, move your pieces as far as you can get them, and then accept that you may have to wait for follow-up before you get the information you need to complete your tasks. So yes, this does mean you may have to spend your whole first go just resetting or recovering passwords. But that's OK. You're showing up, and you're doing the damn thing.

In absolute best practice, the basic landscape I want you to write down and get a look at includes the following:

YOUR INCOME. This may be as simple as taking a good look at a couple of pay stubs, if you're employed, or as complicated as having to do the last year of bookkeeping that you've been putting off for your small business.

YOUR SPENDING. If you're already using a budget-tracking app, great. If not, take a look at minimum three months of bank statements and credit card statements. Don't forget about other accounts, such as Venmo or PayPal.

YOUR DEBT. Make a list of how much you owe, to whom, what the minimum monthly payments are, and what the interest rate is. Bonus points for figuring out exactly how much you're paying in interest on each account monthly. Often this is enough to light a fire to get something paid off faster, and it will definitely help you understand why your accounts take so long to pay down.

YOUR ASSETS. What do you own? This includes retirement accounts from old random jobs, savings accounts, trusts, your car, a house or property, and so on. Write down how much each asset is worth and whether it is liquid or not (this means, is it cash or is it something you would have to sell in order to make it cash).

YOUR CREDIT REPORT. Don't get caught up in which of the different reports to pull, just pick one or, even easier, use an online app that consolidates and reports the information for you. You want to know what your score is and what basic conditions are impacting it. Are your credit cards maxed out? Are all your accounts pretty new? Have you never really established any credit accounts? You can go from figuring out the specific issues to strategizing about raising your score.

Do not stress. You don't have to do all this to stay on track in the book, and I know and trust you will get to this part when you're ready. I want you to know these things so you can get clarity and take ownership of them. Eventually, you will be able to meld the emotional work we're going to do in the rest of the book with this practical data, and then you will be unstoppable!

YOUR INNER LANDSCAPE: CULTIVATING FINANCIAL SELF-AWARENESS

All right, we got the practical thing done. So what does it look like to observe and inventory your inner financial landscape? A large part of this work is noticing the clues that your subconscious mind is offering you in order to understand yourself better. Better understanding means greater self-awareness, and that's going to give us all the information we need about why your financial life is experiencing challenge and where you're working from in the process to evolve.

The entire idea of attempting to tap into your subconscious mind may be new to you. Start to notice what you are saying through your behavior, your feelings, and your thoughts. Behavior is communication. Paying attention to the messages you are sending out from your inner self is a deep form of self-care. Dig underneath the obvious to the underlying significance. For example, regularly buying more groceries than you can realistically consume is a message from your subconscious that you don't feel secure or safe and you are concerned with scarcity. Online shopping for treats that you can't afford may be a message that you feel underappreciated and devalued.

The subconscious mind is the powerful secondary system that basically runs everything in your life. It holds so much more information than we could ever keep track of consciously. It captures everything we've seen, heard, sensed, and felt, whether we "remember" it or not. And it impacts the ways we act and move in this world. Learning how to activate the communication between the conscious and the subconscious minds is a powerful tool to employ on the way to success and abundance. Strengthening this connection is the purpose of all those things we engage to try to find the solitude and calm we need to access our deepest knowing, such as meditation, visualization, divination, journaling, yoga, and getting out in nature.

Self-awareness has two parts:

INTERNAL SELF-AWARENESS is your capacity to recognize your emotional state and the behaviors that stem from it, as well as your capacity to engage tactics to regulate both your emotions and your behavior.

EXTERNAL SELF-AWARENESS is a cognizance of how others may see you and how your actions and behaviors are perceived.

If you're just beginning this type of work, your first step is going to be to strengthen your observational self. Our inner observer is the part of us who will help us develop self-awareness, through monitoring our thoughts, feelings, and actions with objectivity. Imagine a mini you with a clipboard and a hard hat, ready to get trained on the job. It might feel awkward, but everybody's got to start from somewhere, and it's important to understand that we don't have this observing self unless we develop it. To train your inner observer, incorporate a couple of basic self-exploratory practices into your life. Use mindfulness meditation, building the observational mind by focusing on things you usually wouldn't notice: your breathing, how different parts of your body feel, what your mind does when you sit still. As you go about your days, stop to reflect on thoughts or actions that arise. Bonus points for writing these reflections down (a.k.a. journaling) and rereading them later. Notice what activates or triggers feelings, thoughts, and reactions, whether they are positive or negative. Sometimes what sets our self-destructive choices in action is as simple as hunger. Are you messing up your finances (not to mention your relationships) because you didn't eat a sandwich?

In your process of observing yourself, don't forget to notice what you're doing well, what you're awesome at, and where you show up for yourself. Self-awareness isn't all about finding the places you're broken; it's also about noticing your strengths, so when you create new habits, you can build off of what already works.

Self-awareness can be hard because it involves being deeply honest and possibly exploring some parts of ourself that we've been avoiding. This can bring up shame, reliving old trauma, overwhelm, and so on. And you know one of the most common places for people to engage in avoidance in their lives? You guessed it, the reason we're all here: finances. The thing about avoidance is that problems almost never go away on their own. Avoidance is a behavior we engage in because we think it will reduce our stress and anxiety, when in fact it causes high levels of subconscious emotional distress, making us anxious, irritable, and depressed. It also disempowers us, impacts our self-esteem, and causes logistical messes and emergencies we have to clean up later. When I avoid something, I still have to manage the symptoms of the problem in my day-to-day life. I will still be living with that poor credit score or paying to get my car out of impound because I had too many unpaid parking tickets. The issue is still demanding my energy and my attention, but all that energy is flowing toward managing the symptoms rather than exploring the possibility of healing the root cause of my financial woes. The unhealed parts of our finances make (often harsh) demands on us every single day.

Don't forget to take your relative position of societal privilege into consideration when doing self-observation work. The more privilege you experience, the greater the chance that you will have an underdeveloped lens of self-awareness, particularly external self-awareness (understanding accurately how you are perceived and your impact on settings). The

AFFIRMATION

I invite self-awareness into my life. I want to see myself clearly.

more intersecting oppressions you experience, the greater the chance that your lens of external self-awareness has been intensified and focused through the need to stay safe. You may be hyperaware of how you are perceived by other people, including what behaviors are deemed tolerable with regard to the outside world. This can impact your capacity to focus on internal self-awareness. An example of this might be as a woman or a femme attending a family event, you may be so aware of and attuned to other people's subtle reactions to what you are wearing, your hair, your nail style, and your weight that you find great difficulty accurately naming your feelings and tracking whether or not you're taking care of yourself. Afterward, you might end up at home with a huge headache, not totally understanding why you feel unwell.

Whether or not you relate to the experience of being the woman/femme with a people hangover, each one of us is uniquely impacted by capitalist and cultural encouragements to disown our embodied knowledge. Research shows that people typically think they're more self-aware than they demonstrate they are. We can all benefit from putting our attention on our inner experience and upping our financial self-awareness. Look at both your what and your why. This means not just focusing on why you are the kind of person you are, but also considering what kind of person you are.

In order to build your financial self-awareness for the purposes of our journey, here are some things to notice and observe:

YOUR BEHAVIORS. How do you act with money? Do you spend freely or avoid spending? Do you pay bills on time or late? Do you check your bank account balance or just cross your fingers that your card doesn't get declined?

YOUR FEELINGS. How do you feel when you think about, touch, spend, or hear someone talking about money? How do you feel when you get paid? Does it make you anxious, nervous, proud, calm? Notice the connections and similarities between situations that activate certain feelings for you. So if you feel overwhelmed in relationship to money, don't just ask, "Why do I feel so overwhelmed?" but also "What are the situations that make me feel overwhelmed, and what do they have in common?"

YOUR BODY. Reconnect with the feelings and intelligence of your body. The body holds a lot of the information your conscious mind has forgotten. Physical tension can remain in our body in the aftermath of impactful experiences and show itself through sensation. Track the sensations in your body when you interact with the idea of money or money itself. Does your jaw get tight when you get a bill in the mail? Do you feel a flush of shame in your cheeks when you think about how much you earn? This is very valuable information. Pay attention to your energy levels: What drains you, feeds you, fuels you up?

YOUR HISTORY. Make a money time line. Take a sheet of paper and a pencil and, starting at birth, mark the significant financial events of your life along a time line. Write down any event that had a major impact on you, whether big or small. Document both positive and negative events. This could include seemingly big events like a parent losing their job, having to move for financial reasons as a child, getting an amazing scholarship or raise, as well as things that may seem like small occurrences but had a big impact, such as overhearing a parent in distress about money, asking for an important item as a child and being told no, or being given a treat in a store while in full meltdown mode, instead of experiencing what you really needed—your caregiver being attentive to what your needs were in the moment. Reflect on your childhood but also bring your time line up to the current moment.

YOUR LEARNING STYLE. In order to help yourself get to the next level, observe how your brain works and what you need to absorb information or get work done. What motivates you? Write down a list of things that drive you to action. Can you find a way to leverage the things that motivate you to get some change cooking in your financial life? Not everyone learns the same way, and therefore your financial education has to suit you. Think about learning experiences you have enjoyed and feel successful at. Are you visual, auditory, kinesthetic, relational?

Approach learning about money in the same way that you personally and individually learn about anything. Study it like school by reading a book (for example this one, nice work), experience it aurally through a podcast or a video, work with it creatively like your art practice, observe it like an organism if you are an herbalist or a scientist, explore and adventure with it, do it in community, or get a coach or accountability buddy. There is a place for you in money. Take an online test to determine your learning style, and go from there.

YOUR REFLECTION. Get observations from the people around you. If you work with a professional, such as a therapist or coach, ask them to talk to you about money and reflect back what they hear. Another path is asking trusted friends a few questions about how they see your financial behavior. Don't ask vague or open-ended questions, and definitely don't ask shit that you know is going to hurt your feelings or set your loved ones up for you to be mad at them. Make your inquiries clear, specific, and safe for everyone, such as "What do you see me spending the most on?" or "Do I seem uncomfortable when the topic of money comes up?" Don't forget that you may get some feedback you don't like or agree with, or that might challenge your perception of yourself. Be prepared to respond with appreciation and grace. And it has to be consensual. If your beloveds don't want to answer the questions, don't push it or get pouty. The things that annoy and irritate you also offer you a reflection. If something bothers you in someone else, it may be a sign that you have a problem with a similar quality of your own.

YOUR THOUGHTS, BELIEFS, AND BIASES. Make a list of your beliefs about money. Do you believe it is bad, good, neutral? What are your opinions on rich people? Poor people? Unemployed people? Is there a certain salary number you can't ever imagine surpassing?

You know, just some fluffy, casual stuff. Insert tears pouring down my face emoji here.

DON'T SACRIFICE YOUR SOVEREIGNTY TO YOUR PATTERNS

Let's touch back on a point we discussed earlier: Not all your financial problems are due to your personality, your parent's quirks, or your idiosyncratic behavioral choices. Systemic financial oppression, doled out along racial, ethnic, geographic, and gender lines, is real and deeply impacts your financial life. This can look like having possession of stolen resources through inheritance or having your labor devalued and being underpaid at work due to your race or gender. Or both. No amount of self-awareness work overrides or erases intentional systemic financial oppression, nor should you ever be pressured into taking responsibility for the impact of systemic oppression on your finances. You should, however, absolutely feel pressure to take responsibility for the impact of systemic privilege on your finances. Again, this book focuses on what you do have control over: your internal experience and the ways you participate in disempowering yourself. Identifying the line between those things, and riding your personal edge, is key to maximizing your sovereignty.

Even as adults, it might frustratingly feel like we have no control over our environment, and to a certain degree that's true. We have a small field of choice in this world. We don't have control, but we do have agency; our job is to maximize it and not give it away. It is crucial to acknowledge, identify, and reinforce the places where we have agency. The work of this book is to identify the sphere of your own agency.

The stronger we build that self-awareness muscle, the more clearly we will see where we reengage old patterns of behavior when we respond to current situations in an attempt to attain control or success. This is called iteration. Building a skill set and toolbox of self-awareness can help us notice the ways we are replaying out patterns of trauma, earlier reactions, and outdated ways of being in our financial lives. When we gain awareness of a pattern, we can then start noticing it when it plays out. If we can notice it, we have a chance to interject a moment of space in the pattern, slow it down, and, fingers crossed, disrupt the pattern enough to revolutionize the way we respond. When we begin to notice our relationships with structures, policies, and practices, we more clearly see the boundary between where our agency has been taken away from us and where we participate in giving it away.

FINANCIAL GASLIGHTING IS A THING

Our agency is compromised by structural limitations. Without getting too academic, this means that our own individual capacity to make free decisions hits up against blocks imposed by society. So for example, if you come from a low-income family with no financial safety net, you might not be able to work the radical activist job you would like to have because you need to stay in a corporate framework with solid healthcare benefits. It is valuable to both our personal sanity and collective healing processes to acknowledge and visibilize the limitations that exist. This means acknowledging to ourselves, and acknowledging in community, what these oppressions are, what they look like in our material and financial lives, naming them, and planning with them in mind.

This also means not gaslighting ourselves and not gaslighting each other. The term *gaslighting* refers to a type of manipulation where the

AFFIRMATION

I am compassionate toward my coping mechanisms, but I do not enable them.

manipulator tries to get someone else (or a group of people) to question their own reality, memory, or perceptions. Like all forms of deception, it can be done consciously or subconsciously, by individuals and groups. And like most forms of control, it is generally concealed and denied.

Gaslighting behaviors can be inherited and perpetuated through family lines and cultural heritages. There is social and cultural gaslighting around money. Those of us raised in the so-called United States, or in other colonial projects, have been raised in a web of obfuscations about money and how money works that support a faulty and violent narrative. This is the myth of the American dream in all its parts: the myth of bootstrapping, the myth of equal opportunity for success, the myth of meritocracy, the myth of pioneering.

There can also be family gaslighting around money. If you grew up in a household where you were told one thing about money but were able to see a different truth with your own eyes, you may have a more challenging time discerning your financial reality in adulthood. Take a look at your upbringing: Were there hard truths about money that your family, community, or institutions around you were intentionally obscuring, such as being told "there's no money for that" when you need something for school while simultaneously watching a shopping- or gambling-addicted parent spend money freely? Your parents may not have been able, or ready, or willing to face hard truths. You may have suffered as a result of this. They also may have intentionally trained you to avoid the truth by gaslighting you, by silencing you when you spoke the truth, by punishing you for resisting, by shaming you when they felt embarrassed. We can be groomed into family patterns of manipulation and codependence by being looped in to propping up the delusions of our family members. It may have been our job to make sure other people are comfortable. We may have been shown that if we don't make people comfortable, they will take their love or material support away from us. As kids, this is life-threatening. In adulthood, it still sucks, to be honest.

Sometimes we even gaslight ourselves to justify denying a truth we don't want to or aren't ready to see. Notice where you've developed habits of obscuring your financial information and truth from yourself, even casually. These habits of mind are inherited and easy to slip into. They may even seem harmless, until you realize you're undermining your own sanity. Saying "I'm so broke" when you have money in the bank, telling yourself you don't have money to go to the dentist when you are spending equivalent money at Target, or telling yourself you can afford something nonessential when it means you'll have to put it on a credit card are all examples of this behavior.

Whether these habits of delusion play a role in your family's money story or not, healing from financial gaslighting is essential work, as we are all being exposed on a societal level. Speaking and listening to truth telling about economic realities is key—in your family, in your workplace, in your nation, and in your personal finances. Support your desire to understand your finances better, even if it's a quiet or small part of how you feel. Build trust with yourself and listen to your feelings and opinions, especially if you are experiencing marginalization. It's OK to feel confusion or doubt when you're learning to center your own perception. Giving kindness and compassion to your confusion will allow you to stay present with the feeling long enough that you can move through it toward clarity and direction. All the exercises in this chapter are designed to help you see and understand your own experience more clearly. Take the time to really ground and center in the information that you find, trusting that you can handle the truth.

Reclaim your sanity, stand in the truth of what you see clearly, and arm yourself with your own financial facts, your numbers, and your self-awareness. If people in your life aren't trustworthy, or you know they are invested in their own mess, don't let them comment on or influence your financial goals or decision-making. You are an adult, you are the ruler of your own life, and you are a beloved and honorable ancestor in the making. Be accountable to the souls of your descendants, whether they be by birth or by choice. Do the work now to lay the ground for a more healed and liberated future. Commit to being a badass babe who's not afraid of yourself or afraid of the truth!

RITUAL

Past, Present, and Future

This spiritual bathing ritual draws on the purifying element of water and the wisdom of the Jewish tradition of mikveh in order to release the past, arrive in the present, and bless the future.

You may either do this in a tub or standing in your shower or outside. If you are using a tub, you will do three full dunks under the water and focus on the intentions of one step with each dunk. If you are using the shower or outdoors method, fill a bucket with water, and bring a smaller, quart-size (960 ml) vessel for pouring. With the emotional intention of each step, pour a full vessel of water over your head and each shoulder.

Intention 1: Release the Past

Stop carrying the burden of your past mistakes. Forgive yourself entirely for any financial missteps, self-injurious behaviors, and unhealthy habits you have engaged in. Forgive yourself for any debt you have accrued. Let go of the baggage of the past. Leave your judgments of yourself—all the ways you find yourself lacking and any regrets you have. Let it dissolve in the water and wash down the drain. List out loud the behaviors you are leaving behind.

Intention 2: Arrive in the Present

You are here, now, and you are perfect. You are perfectly where you need to be on your unique human journey.

Intention 3: The Future Is Redemptive

Decide where you are headed, that you are moving toward something better, more aligned, and more healed. Let the water infuse you with the power of hope. Give yourself a second chance.

STEP

3

Figure Out What You Want, What You Really, Really Want

Identify your true financial desires, and then refine them into real-life goals.

MONEY MAGIC ALLIES

Astrological Role Models

Taurus and Leo: These signs want to be right in the middle of everything that looks good, feels good, smells good, and sounds good. Wanting only good things for yourself and those around you means tapping in to what just feels good and resonates, without worrying too much about the how and the why. When we elevate our life by aligning with the things that truly make us happy and comfortable, we radiate a special vibration of walking in purpose. When we stop denying what we really want and who we truly are, we can integrate, bringing our integrity, ethics, and discernment into alignment with our desires and our purpose.

Crystal Friends

Citrine: Citrine is the stone for manifesting financial freedom. Citrine elevates you and removes fear and anxiety. This sunny yellow-orange gem, sometimes called the lucky merchant stone, helps you manifest from a place of deep-rooted self-esteem, boosting your will to take advantage of opportunities and elevate your financial success in business. It helps accumulate wealth but also helps you protect what you've already acquired, so it can be a good stone to prevent overspending or financial disaster.

Pyrite: Pyrite is the go-to mineral for manifesting wealth. It's highly energetic and embodies the vitality of abundance and success. It helps clear blockages that are interfering with your manifestation process, projecting negative energies back from whence they came in the same fashion as a mirror or an evil eye charm. Sometimes called fool's gold, this disco ball–like mineral attracts money and luck when worn or carried on the body. If you want a better financial future, make friends with pyrite.

Tiny Tarot Reading

The Sun: Let the wisdom of your heart shine brightly in everything you do! You know what's good for you, and you walk firmly in the light. Your shadows do not scare you and you feel no need to avoid them, knowing they are only showing you where you need to shine your light. As you illuminate a problem, you intuit how to solve it and the solution brings you joy. You are filled with a sense of purpose and knowledge that comes straight from a divine source, and you know that everything on Earth is also filled with this divine light. Abundance fills every corner of your life. Good things are attracted to your bright energy. Clarity and direction come to you with ease.

Cup of Tea

Hibiscus, calendula, and hawthorn berry with honey will open the desires of the heart and call in sunshine and abundant sweetness.

This chapter's the fun one. This is where we're figuring out our destination, deciding where we want to be headed on our journey to a more magical relationship with money. Think of it like planning a vacation for your finances.

We're going to make space to really identify our financial desires. This means taking ownership of our desires: seeing who we really are, what we really want, and letting ourselves want it. This means taking responsibility for our desires, knowing we are the only ones who are going to get us what we want in this world, so we better get real clear on what it is. Don't waste your precious life just going along with other folks' plans and taking what comes your way. You are allowed to want more for yourself.

Letting yourself want something—or more precisely, letting yourself acknowledge and see that you want something—will stop your subconscious mind from getting in the mix and messing it all up. You are reading this book because you want to turn toward money and perhaps wealth with purpose and integrity. You want to feel different and reduce your anxiety about money. You're done with the struggle.

A lot of us are conditioned not to ask for too much and not to get bigger than the people around us. From birth we're constantly told what we should want, what's good for us, and what's considered dangerous. Some of the people who dictated our desires were trying to protect us, some of them were trying to control us, and it's safe to say most of them weren't coming from a place of liberatory self-awareness. Conversely, you may have been taught that it's your exclusive responsibility to get more, to be more successful, and to gather financial resources to share with the rest of your family. You may have been taught that making any personal choices that deviate from the family plan is unacceptable and selfish. Figuring out what you personally want wasn't necessarily part of the plan.

What is your reason for reading this book? What do you want, and how do you want to feel? What do you want to be different about your life? What do you really, really want? Let's find out. There are so many right paths. The divine reality is that all paths can contain good and you must choose only the one that is truest to you. Your soul has to journey your road, the one that takes you where you want to go. There is no one-size-fits-all life, and therefore there is no-one-size-fits-all path to financial success.

In this step, you'll learn some techniques to identify and validate your financial desires in order to make a financial plan that truly excites you.

PERMISSION GRANTED: CLAIMING FINANCIAL AUTHORITY

We've been taught that we need the approval of an authority figure in our finances, and I have noticed that sometimes clients come to me seeking permission to make a particular money move. I imagine some of you reading this book are also looking for that, so let me give it to you. Permission granted. If you've done your homework, and you're acting in self-awareness, then I support you. But has anyone ever told you that you need to become your own financial authority? This doesn't mean never seek advice or education; on the contrary, good leaders know they need regular, continuing education and counsel. And it's very normal to want some consistent validation and reality testing from trusted third parties. But you're the adult and you need to sign your own permission slip.

So much of our beliefs and desires about money have been formed either to mirror or be in rebellion to our family's financial mindset. We think we need to be like them, or we absolutely do not want to be anything like them. Either way, our motivation is reactionary and not grounded in our unique self. Think back to the time line we made in step 2. What does it tell you about your family's money story? Think of the people who raised you. How would you describe their outlooks on money? Are there any expressions about money you heard over and over in childhood that stick in your head? Go back a generation. Who raised the people who raised you? What are their money stories and what did they pass on? In the midst of all these inherited ideas, can you locate what a self-loving relationship with money looks like?

You are entitled to a financial plan that centers your individual desires and values. Your financial plan should excite you, not feel like a half-assed attempt at being an adult. A lot of what we think of as our financial desires and ideas are created out of fear, scarcity, and grasping for approval. When we are force-fed one-size-fits-all financial education, making a money plan can seem more like taking your vitamins, just something to do to be a good person. It's not necessarily the kind of self-care that feels satisfying or fun. Making a budget or figuring out how to save for retirement as a self-employed person just doesn't have that same "treat yourself" vibe as taking a bubble bath. But making your relationship with money more easeful is an incredible act of self-love and care. Take the time to clarify what your values are and what your desires are. Build your plan from there. Yes, incorporate the bits of good advice you've gotten along the way. Yes, pay attention to what works for other people and might work for you. Yes, get informed about the boring details of things that impact your life, such as taxes, your 401(k), and how to improve your credit score. But ground and center in what you want, not what other people have told you that you should want. Turning those shoulds into wants might make all the difference in actually leveling up successfully.

The key to shifting out of the conform-or-rebel pattern is to mature! Take responsibility for figuring out what you want, put your back into it, and get invested. Mature desires are much sexier anyway. Taking responsibility doesn't sound like the funnest, but it becomes easier when you feel like it's your idea and you have buy-in. The idea of buy-in comes from organizational, educational, and corporate culture—how do you get participants to really be emotionally invested in the success of an endeavor or project? It's an idea worth considering as you explore why you may not have been invested in previous attempts at financial self-care. Were you doing it for someone else, but not yourself? If you don't perceive a plan as truly serving you, it's hard to follow through with it with joy and motivation. Commit to making your financial plans from a place of authenticity rather than performing financial maturity to gain approval.

Sometimes there are more insidious reasons for not following through. Self-sabotage definitely can rear its head. A part of you actually may be invested in financial change not working out so that you can stay comfortable or reinforce a story you have about yourself. Self-punishment can also occur. You block yourself from success because a part of you feels like you don't deserve it, either due to long-standing shame or because you're punishing yourself for past mistakes. Judging your past can result in doling out punishments to yourself. Internalizing other people's judgments of you can keep you stuck and feeling undeserving. Do you feel like you deserve to be punished for past mistakes? Do you believe that you deserve financial stability?

JOURNAL PROMPT
Values Clarification

Write a list of three people you look up to financially. What actions do they take that you admire? What material success have they achieved that you feel attracted to, or even envious of?

Make a second list titled "Why Money Is Important to Me." Brainstorm anything and everything that comes up. It's OK if the first time you try, you just write, "It's not." Or you get frustrated or angry. Keep looping back to this list as you come up with new thoughts and ideas.

YOUR DESIRES ARE DIVAS

I'm going to guess I'm not the only diva reading this book. You know we do not like to be ignored. The better you treat a diva, the more outrageously fabulous they are going to become. Take your desires seriously. Divas hate to be repressed. We hate to be boxed in or told we're too big or there's no space for us. Your desires feel the same way! They are tired of being told they're too much, especially when you haven't spent the time to really get to know them. Divas hate to be misunderstood and unseen.

Technically, a diva is a big-time female opera star and has been a compliment reserved for the greatest singers in the world. In pop vernacular, *diva* is often used derogatorily for high-maintenance women to imply entitlement and narcissism. Misogyny is, like, so obvious. So here's the deal: Let's stop internalizing shame about our inner diva and let's stop internalizing shame about having and prioritizing desires. Thank the Goddess for Beyoncé's iconic reclamation of the word in her 2008 anthem "Diva."

The desires of feminine and feminized people are belittled as superfluous, fantastical, frivolous. Exploitation culture also thrives on viewing the desires of marginalized people as nonexistent or base. You may have been groomed to center what other people want, to anticipate others' needs and provide for them. Your nervous system may have formed a vigilance to the needs of others around you through growing up in a household where abuse, addiction, or alcoholism was present. If you grew up being expected to take care of others in this way, it often goes hand in hand that your own desires and needs were repressed and invisibilized.

Desire is powerful. We may have been taught that our desires are too powerful, that they're dangerous and we can't trust ourselves for wanting them. This is the most harmful kind of messaging because it erodes our internal compass. It pushes us to trust other people instead of ourselves as "experts" on our own lives. It gaslights us into being unable to make decisions. We may have been told that our desires are too big, not to mention our personalities, our curiosities, our need for truth, our emotions, and our bodies. We find all sorts of ways to make ourselves smaller and less self-determined. We box ourselves in, limiting ourselves in order to be more palatable. We spread ourselves too thin so that the full concentration of ourself is never threatening to those we love or those we depend on for survival. Then it becomes a habit.

Letting your desires take center stage can be a lifestyle (hello, Leos) or it can be an exercise. But we are not going to shame, minimize, or ignore our desires anymore. Having big desires and being willing to hustle hard to live in alignment with those desires is not "doing too much." Knowing what you want and how to communicate it clearly in a loving but boundaried way is a gift not only to yourself but also to those around you. The shadow side comes when we can't compromise or when we're unable to acknowledge other people's efforts, when we try to mold or push others to conform their desires to ours in a partnership or collective setting, or when we don't have a good sense of when it's appropriate to center our desires and when it's appropriate to compromise. It can also look like blaming others when we don't get what we want, instead of having the grace to accept it as a normal part of life. A self-aware and secure diva is confident in their abilities and contributions, and they love recognition—but they are happy to give credit to others too.

JOURNAL PROMPT
The Power of Desire

How were desires treated within your family structure growing up? Were you taught that your desires were valuable? Harmful? Irrelevant? Overwhelming?

When you were given things or opportunities that you desired, were they given to you with gentleness? Resentment? Did these opportunities come with attached expectations that seemed high stakes?

MINDFULNESS MOMENT

Experience Abundance

Release scarcity, embrace abundance. Scarcity is the belief that you are not enough and there is not enough. It can also be the belief that things are for other people but not for you. Abundance is the belief that there is enough and you are deserving.

Sit comfortably and breathe deeply, noticing the physical feeling of breath entering your body, filling your lungs, and releasing out. Breathe in to the count of three, repeating in your mind, *There is enough*. Breathe out to the count of three, repeating in your mind, *I am deserving*.

THE VULNERABILITY OF DESIRE

Desire is vulnerable. I get it; I hate to be disappointed, and I hate to feel foolish. Really wanting something opens you up to the heartbreak of it not happening. When too many things have not gone the way you hoped they would, it's easy to feel unsafe wanting, hoping, and wishing. Sitting in a place of desire may be new and uncomfortable. Longing can be painful. Having things and then losing them adds a whole other layer. It may have been a long time since you let yourself really want something or feel hope that things could change. You might need to cry it out.

What does your heart deeply desire? Do you give your heart space to speak freely, without censorship? What have you previously considered impossible? What are the desires that whisper to you quietly, that are sitting in the back of the classroom?

In their highest form, desires can propel us through the fears and blocks that stop us from living freely. That's the work of this process to a more magical relationship with money: successfully navigating those blocks, fueled by desire and self-awareness. It's important to really locate your desires, because it's the power of that desire that is going to create the momentum to push through when the blocks get hard. It's emotional physics!

We harden our hearts to our true desires and replace them with the success signposts of capitalism. Or we replace them with creature comforts. Our financial desires are more than just things we want to have. In a consumerist culture, we are conditioned to want things, without always having an accurate read on why we want them. We want items and experiences that we hope will soothe our unfilled needs. These "comforts" have been peddled to us by a society unable or unwilling to take our real needs seriously. Because of this conditioning, it may take us a little digging to move beyond superficial wants to our deeper, more holistic and fulfilling desires. If you haven't learned how to listen to your real needs, you may have struggled to see or accept your true desires, ignoring or invalidating them. Explore the core desires that lie underneath the creature-comfort wants. When you desire an object, or desire to go shopping, look underneath to see whether the core desire might be to feel secure or safe, in control, pretty or attractive, distracted from emotional pain, rewarded, deserving, comforted, or loved.

It's a lot easier to want a glass of wine than to want deep intimacy, community, fulfillment. The experience of finding things out of grasp can get so tiring that we stop reaching altogether. And that's OK. Your arms are tired. Your heart may be tired too. But give it some space, give it some permission, give it some room to dream. How big do you want to stretch, how free do you want to be? All our heart's desires probably do not center around money, but our economic desires are important, and many of our desires do have an economic side. Desire for stability may involve paying for the perfect house for you and your family. Desire

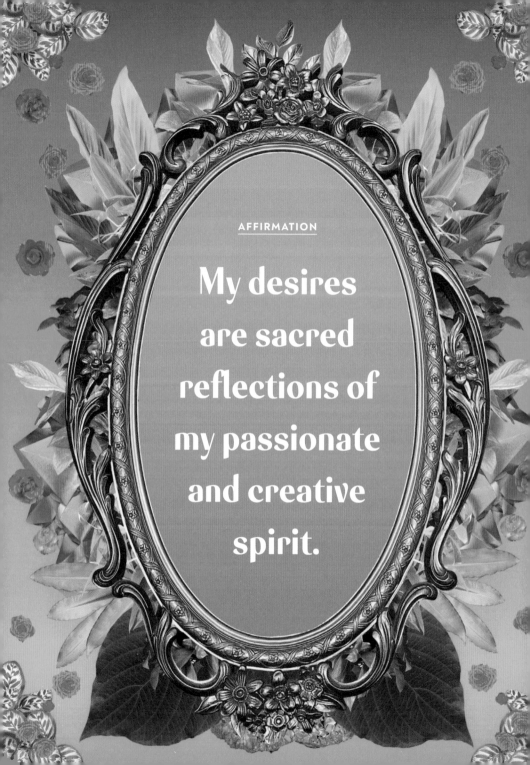

AFFIRMATION

My desires are sacred reflections of my passionate and creative spirit.

for community might involve buying land. Desire for independence and sovereignty is always helped by the infamous "fuck it" fund, which means cultivating a savings account that can permit you to walk away from unhealthy jobs or relationships. Rather than getting frustrated or discouraged by the economic aspect of your dreams, get curious and excited about where the funds will come from and how they will perfectly align in your life in a way that supports, nurtures, and enables your big dreams to happen.

HEAL YOUR FINANCES HOMEWORK

Money Witch Savings Challenge

Cultivate a savings practice, no matter how small. Saving $20 per week will yield $1,040 at the end of the year. This will allow you to buy a new computer, do a wardrobe overhaul, put a little something toward retirement or a down payment on a used car, get major car repairs or new tires, or launch a new product for your side hustle.

Make sure to build in the technology of how it will happen: How much will you save per week or pay period? Where will you save it (bank account, safe, envelope)? How will you easefully transfer the money each week?

I want to acknowledge here that when I talk about cold hard cash in this book, as an author from the so-called United States, I refer to US dollars. I use these exercises because I think it is helpful to have tangible, numbers-based examples to reflect on. These tools are for you no matter where you live, if you want them. Take a moment to reflect on the example, bringing in your own currency for relevance.

THE REVOLUTIONARY
POWER OF DREAMING

The first thing our mind does when we sleep is heal and digest the subconscious mind's experience of day-to-day life. Then we connect to messages, visions, information, solutions, and contributions that will help us move forward with our purpose. The dream state is healing, and it has information for you. Use your dreams, both your nighttime ones and your daydreams, to give you insight on your desires. Empress Karen Rose, owner of Sacred Vibes Apothecary in Brooklyn, New York, said in her 2020 keynote speech at the Spiritual Herbalism Conference, "Dream state is the new woke. We gain another form of sight when we dream." Much of the work of identifying your desires is just making an inviting space for them to land. Invite your most outlandish dreams, desires, and fantasies to move out of your subconscious and into your waking life. Get out of my dreams and into my car.

One of the most powerful things about making space to be dreamy is that it allows you to play with ideas about money without feeling immediate pressure to manifest or comply. Money is obviously serious, but you are allowed to mess around and try things out before you get down to the business of making a plan. In fact, this is sort of essential. Giving yourself leeway to go down financial fantasy rabbit holes will expand your concept of what is possible. This doesn't mean just daydream a bunch of different scenarios where you don't have to take responsibility and you get rescued out of your financial mess. Imagining more for yourself also means imagining a you who is responsible and conscientious with money. Explore and find the biggest version of yourself, the richest version of yourself, the poorest version of yourself, the bossest version of yourself, the most generous version of yourself, the most fiscally conservative version of yourself. Play out the scenarios in your mind and notice what feels exciting and what feels motivating. Those are clues to your core desires.

JOURNAL PROMPT

Daydreaming

Take some time to trip out on the following questions:

In terms of money, what would I like to have that I don't have now?

If I had that, was that, or could do that, what would it give me and how would it make me feel?

Explore and dream underneath each answer, to find the real root.

TOOLS FOR TUNING IN TO YOUR SUBCONSCIOUS DESIRES

As you'll remember from step 2, the key to a lot of the information we need is accessing our subconscious mind. Besides dreamwork, there are many other tools designed to help you bring your desires to the light of day:

PEACE, MAN. Try to find some peaceful space every day, even if just for two minutes. Cultivate moments of calm in your life in order to quiet your conscious mind. Put on some soothing music, take some deep breaths, and shake off the immediate layer of stress and chatter that bubbles up. Utilize soothing sounds, scents, and colors to calm the chatter of your nervous system and tap into a deeper layer of your psyche.

SPACE OUT. Staring into space is a completely underrated to-do list item. Having some time to just listen to your mind with no clear agenda is actually essential to success. Utilize meditation, chanting, visualization, or other techniques designed to help surprising ideas emerge from the corners of your mind. Notice and validate any synchronicities or aha moments that arise in your day-to-day life.

ACTIVATE ART AND CREATIVITY. Make a vision board or a collage of pictures that exemplify your money desires, and see what patterns you notice or what words come to mind when you look at it. Stream-of-consciousness writing, freedrawing, and painting can also give you space to express freely. Try working on a piece called "Abundance," "Wealth," "Prosperity," or "Desire," and see what comes.

DIVINE INTERVENTION. Start engaging a divination practice. Across cultures, your ancestors have created these practices, and there are so many readers, teachers, priestesses, magicians, and practitioners out there putting a modern spin on them. You might resonate with pulling tarot or oracle cards, the symbolism of rune stones, gazing into obsidian or other crystals, reading coffee grounds or tea leaves, pendulum dowsing, throwing I Ching, receiving Ifa divination, or throwing bones or shells. All systems of divination are designed to help you access information from your subconscious, your highest spiritual self, and the rest of the spirit world. Remember that pulling information from your subconscious or the spirit realm into your conscious mind is energy-intensive, and treat yourself like you did something exhausting. Make time to rest and also to receive nurturing after you engage these practices.

USE YOUR JEALOUSY AS A TOOL. When you feel jealous of someone or something, take note and take it seriously. You're not a terrible person for coveting your neighbor's apartment just a little. What's not cool is repressing our own desires and projecting that repression onto others by turning our jealousy into judgment. I mean, if it's just flat-out judgment, then go at it (I can't suspend my critical mind either), but do yourself the favor of exploring if you're really pushing away something you want and demonizing it because you feel like you can't have it. Don't forget to dig underneath the initial jealousy to see what it symbolizes to you. You might not want someone's career-track job that requires them to work sixty hours a

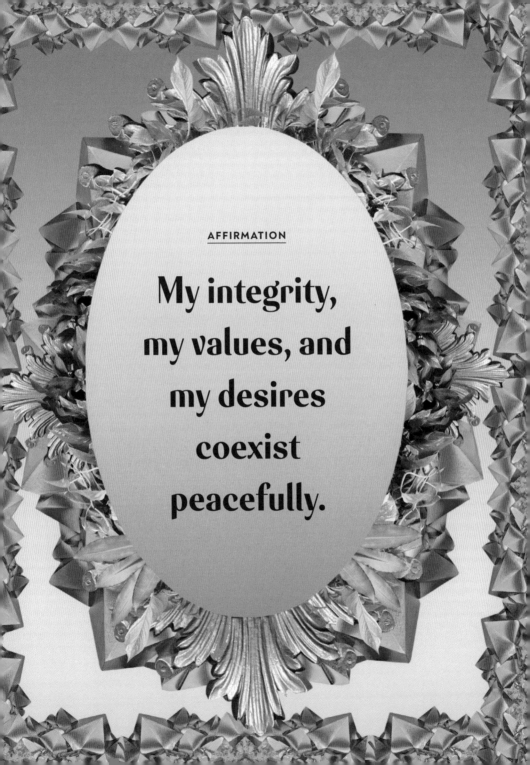

AFFIRMATION

My integrity, my values, and my desires coexist peacefully.

week, but you may be jealous of their capacity to purchase quality, meaningful items for their home. You might not want to move out of your coastal city to buy a four-bedroom home in the Midwest like your friend just did, but you may have a deep desire for space, privacy, and agency in your housing. Excavate your jealousies and your judgments to find the treasure of your core desires.

ACCOUNTABILITY: POLITICS, PRIVILEGE, AND DESIRE

Focusing on your own desires can bring up guilt and confusion. How can I want more when others have less? How can I make space for my own desires when so many people worldwide are struggling to literally just stay alive and fed?

Here is a very painful truth: There is no possible way to reconcile the idea of human suffering. As tempting as it is to grasp for a sense of control within the world of capitalism, it is important to recognize a few things. Often we hold on to disarming ideas like if you have less, others will have more. In most cases, that's not actually true. Yes, share what you have, especially with people who are experiencing current or historical marginalization that you're not. Yes, redistribute hoarded colonial wealth. But you wearing a torn hand-me-down winter coat for three more years than you want or need to will not alleviate human suffering. It will not ease the psychological burden and realities many of us face. You overdrafting your account because you don't want to focus on making more money because it's "capitalist" helps no one.

Another painful truth: You can't tap out of capitalism. And that means that for most of us, there's no such thing as ethical earning, housing, or consumption. Be responsible instead. You should absolutely strive to make accountable choices within that reality, but you will waste a ton of energy if your goal is to do something that is impossible.

I get the most political pushback at this stage of the process. Like, is it really OK for people to want anything they want? What if my human desires are too big, too consumptive, exploitative? In some ways, your exploration of your desires may take you into your shadow side a little. That is OK; suppressing our desires just makes them land mines in our real life. When we get clear about our desires, then we can make conscious decisions about how we want to incorporate them into our lives. Acknowledging our desires doesn't mean we want to be unaccountable. Fear of money and fear of wealth are really fears of yourself. The fear that if you become wealthy or well resourced you will become a bad person is based on a belief that you are inherently bad and the only thing that redeems you is poverty or being under-resourced. Whether or not you were raised in a family or religious community that told you money was bad and evil, the idea of original sin permeates Western imagination, and we are not exempt from soaking that up.

I remember teaching this desire step at a workshop a while back in Oakland, California, and I used the example that ever since I was a kid, I've wanted a Corvette (like Barbie had, duh). A student was questioning the ethics of acting on that desire—is it really OK to get a Corvette if that's what you want? And here's where we need to check ourselves to see where we are truly creating impact and where we are virtue signaling. We engage signifiers that emblemize our ethics more often to gain comfort and approval from our peers than to actually change the societies we live in. Like is it more ethical for me to drive a 2010 Subaru than a 2010 Corvette? No, I doubt that it is. But it does allow me to signify liberal values. Take a hard look at where you compromise your desires out of a wish to have real impact and where you are compromising them in order to flag "good person" within a certain subculture. Check in and audit where your discomfort with embracing your desires is coming from.

Additionally, just because you realize you want something does not mean you have to pursue it. The process of discernment is a key part of maturity. Just don't confuse repression and denial for refinement. You get to take your politics with you on your journey to financial healing. You

AFFIRMATION

I am a well-resourced person who helps resource others.

get to take your ethics with you. You get to take your integrity with you. So yeah, if the truth is that you're actually a shitty person, then you may be in trouble. But I doubt that's true. Integrity is really the key concept. Remember back from step 1 that integrity means aligning your actions with your values. We fear that our compassion, our belief in mutual aid, and a just peace is based in staying financially marginalized. I see this fear predominantly in clients who have race privilege, specifically white clients, particularly if they also grew up with some class privilege, even if it was the lower middle class. This attitude can also be cultivated by spending time in certain subcultures, such as punk or activist spaces. Low economic status is one of the only experiences of marginalization that can be actively pursued. We believe that if we have enough resources to live a middle-class life, then we won't relate to or care about the experiences of marginalized people anymore. But if these are really your values, you will demonstrate that by aligning your behavior with them no matter what your access to resources is.

Spending time thinking and learning about money, how to make more of it, and how to save, build, and invest in your community's future will not take any more time away from your work in this world than you're currently spending worrying about money. The movement doesn't need more broke people.

Sacred Sleep and Dream Incubation

At certain points in time and space, sacred sleep has been a world-wide religious practice. Activating sacred dreaming technology in your life helps you strengthen the connection between your conscious and subconscious mind. Ancient and Indigenous cultures have rituals and techniques to harness the power of this information. Just like all "alternative" ways of being, dreams and the sleep state have been honored and deeply valued by societies that value holistic ways of knowing while being devalued and minimized by kyriarchal ones. Reclaim sacred sleep and the value and power of the information available to you in your liminal state, as you travel between worlds. Dreams help you process the experiences of your day and access information from your subconscious mind via symbolism. Psychic or telepathic dreaming may bring you messages from other dimensions, such as the future. Spirit(s) may choose to communicate their directives and advice to you through dreams. Dreams can also be a form of journeying into other realms—traveling in time and space in a way our physical form cannot, similar to psychedelic journeying.

Dream reality is an important liminal and altered state. In dream incubation, we use sleep as a ritual to intentionally create sacred dreams for a specific purpose: for healing, for a solution to a problem, for advice, to request a specific blessing. In this case, your goal is to create sacred dreams with the intention of understanding your truest, fullest financial desires. This ritual may be particularly potent when the moon is full, or when the moon is in Aries, Leo, or Taurus.

Honor your dream time by practicing sleep hygiene. Sleep hygiene means creating a routine and an environment that promote consistent, uninterrupted sleep. Having a regular pre-sleep routine can help you fall asleep more easily and more soundly. Drink a cup of soothing tea—herbs, such as chamomile, lavender, lemon balm, and kava, can help your body and mind relax. Giving yourself time to wind down (without screens or electronics), dimming your lights, and using a relaxation technique like meditation, breathing exercises, or yoga can all contribute to good sleep hygiene. Clear your mind by journaling or consciously releasing your worries.

Before you sleep, say a prayer for accessing your deepest desires. You can write this request on a paper and slip it inside your pillowcase or put it on your altar. You can petition out loud. Ask the Universe to open your heart and mind, to release all preconceived notions of yourself, to expand your limited view of what is possible, and to show you your true desires.

Get a cute notebook or journal and pen to keep at your bedside. Write down any dreams that you have, or any insights that you wake up with. Make sure your notebook is accessible so that you can write in the middle of the night if you need to. A regular routine of dream recollection helps your mind remember more easily. Don't feel bad about pieces that slip away or parts you can't remember. Your dream time is also an important time for your mind to process and digest your experiences, and if you can't remember something, it's because it was not intended as a message for your conscious mind.

Dream big!

STEP

4

Set Your Intention, Let's Go!

Help your desires turn the corner into action.

MONEY MAGIC ALLIES

Astrological Role Model

Virgo: Virgo is the temple priest/ess, the person who is whole unto themselves. In tending to the temple, Virgo understands that many spiritual tasks are mundane. Virgo serves Spirit by sweeping the temple steps, washing the temple cat's water bowl, and keeping the sacred flames lit. As an earth sign, Virgo wants things to be tangible. To bring your dreams to the material realm you have to take your big ideas and narrow them down into a concrete to-do list. Be in sacred service to your financial desires by cutting through the noise to narrow in on the one thing that will have the most impact. Figure out your priorities, act on them, and ignore the rest.

Crystal Friends

Clear Quartz: One of the most ubiquitous and well-known crystals, clear quartz helps you clear the clutter and get real about what your true intention is. No matter what your goals are, clear quartz can help you manifest them, as this stone amplifies your vision outward. Meditate while holding clear quartz to get the clarity and confidence needed to impact the environment around you. Keep clear quartz nearby while you write out all your intentions, affirmations, and goals.

Andalusite: When cut a certain way, graphite particles in andalusite form two black lines that cross in an X-marks-the-spot pattern, making it a very special stone for goal-setting work. Andalusite reminds you that your intention deeply matters and you must always stay aware of where your actions originate. This stone also helps access information from the ancestral and Spirit realms, bringing it into your body as an inner knowing. It helps the messages received be clear and assists you in interpreting them as well.

Tiny Tarot Reading

Chariot and The High Priestess: Keep focused and your dreams will come true. You truly have the power to make it happen through a combination of practical effort and sheer energetic magnetism. Your inner voice will guide you in knowing where you need to go and what you need to do. Tap into what you already know, and stop second-guessing yourself. Reflection is essential, but uncertainty will dilute the potency of your personal power. Pay attention to the wisdom of your heart. Base your actions on love and be disciplined in acting from this place. Focus your intention on the highest good of all involved. Transformation is possible when you concentrate your efforts, so give yourself permission to laser in on actualizing your dreams.

Cup of Tea

Yarrow, mugwort, and chamomile will strengthen intuition while protecting your energetic boundaries.

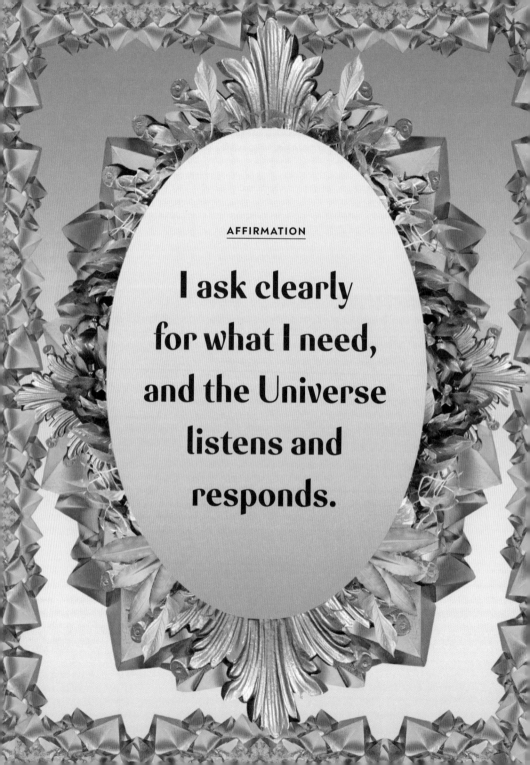

AFFIRMATION

I ask clearly for what I need, and the Universe listens and responds.

All right, we're ready to make moves!

We looked at our lives and our behaviors to figure out where we're currently located, and we dug deep in our subconscious to determine where we'd like to be headed. In this step, we'll create an intention to further refine our direction and set our journey into action. It's like hitting the *get route* button on your energetic GPS. Turn the key in the engine and let's actually get going!

Intention is where desire turns the corner into action. So let's get into the process of creating financial intentions, shaping our desires into the sharp precision of an intention that will cut a clear path for us to travel. We're cultivating agency and sovereignty by fully owning each step, and in this step that means taking responsibility for turning our desires into intentions. The blessings you desire unfold in your actions. You are holding the power of transformation within you, so let's get it focused and get you moving in the direction of your desires.

Moving from a desire to an intention is a process of clarification and discernment. We opened up to the abundance of brainstorming our desires. Now we apply our strategic mind, our politics, our values, and our priorities to distill what it is we are going to put our efforts toward truly creating in our life. Distillation is the process of separating something down into parts to seek its essence, its most potent form. Intention guides you to your most powerful behavior. Appreciate the sharpness and clarity of discernment. Think of it like a breath of cool air, like a knife that slices down and separates what's important from what's a distraction. It is the lightning strike of revelation. Sometimes we resist clarity when the message is not one that we want to hear, but learn to love the sensation of being directed on your path.

The goal of this step is to take all the raw information we unlocked about what we truly want in step 3 and sharpen it into a clear and precise direction for our path.

WHAT IS AN INTENTION?

An intention is a statement that shifts and bends an idea from the realm of desire into the realm of action and possibility, where it cycles from the element of air to the element of earth. When we state an intention, we enter into a deliberate cocreation process with the energetic world. This means we invite the Universe, the Spirits, the ancestors, the angels, the plants, the crystals, and all other parts of the organic and archetypal world that have our backs and want to make something happen for our highest good.

An intention is also a wish. It could be a wish to attract something new or a wish to be free of the traps of your subconscious mind, habits of behavior or thoughts that keep you stuck and work against you. Wishing is a form of healing; it signifies an opening to possibility and the willingness to dream into a potentiality that may be beyond what seems practical. A little impracticality can be a tool when we are learning to let go of limiting beliefs!

An intention is a commitment to yourself and your goals. It's a promise to become more aligned with your highest self and more actualized. The habits and traps that hold us back are developed over our childhoods, our upbringing; they're formed by the unhealed wounds of our family of origin and our ancestral line; and they are formed in past lives, by our spiritual history and travels. Cultivating intention for a shift solidifies a belief that you can evolve further, taking what your lineage has handed you and building it to its next form. Intention may be a commitment to follow a path set for you by Spirit, a form of listening to your guides and agreeing to follow their leadership in your life.

An intention sets a direction for you. It is the compass that reminds you to guide your behavior toward a particular light rather than act out of reaction to the stimulus around you. Guiding your behavior may mean cultivating more of certain behaviors, and divesting from other behaviors, in order to stay on the course you have chosen. Our behavior is largely a set of habits and reactions. The more intentionality we bring to our actions, the more we have the power to change our behavior and the ways we do (or don't) react. As we cultivate a determined sense of clarity, direction, and purpose, we are less impacted by things that would have previously pulled us off course. These could be distractions, perceived injuries, or emotional manipulations that may have at one time felt quite compelling. When we stay clear on where we are headed, and truly desire to be headed there, we're less likely to be seduced by other offers along the way. Don't get distracted by the riffraff.

JOURNAL PROMPT
Paid in Full

Either draw a blank check in your journal or take a blank check from your checkbook. On the line that says "Pay to the order of," write your full name. On the line where you write out the dollar amount, write "Paid in Full." In the little box where you write the numerical dollar amount, write "Paid in Full."

Then sign the check from "The Bank of Abundance," "The Universe," "Infinitely Deserving," or any other source that inspires you. Don't forget to write "Thank you!" in the memo.

INTENTION, INTUITION, AND ENERGETIC HYGIENE

These intentions come from inside you, from your inner knowing. But finding the voice of our intuition may not feel, well, intuitive. Our intuition is only one part of our interiority, our inner experience, so in order to find it, you have to sit there, dig around, and sort out and untangle the voices of your inner experience.

When we're listening in, seeking our inner voice, our intuition, the first thing we may notice as sensitive people is other people's stuff. This can come in the form of voices, thoughts, physical sensations, opinions, and so on. Attuning to our inner compass and making truthful choices becomes difficult when you're not clear on what's yours and what's not. It can really help to develop an energetic hygiene routine and stick to it! It works only if you use it.

When thinking about energetic hygiene, consider your body, your energy field, and your environment. Think about protection when you leave the house and clearing when you come back. Explore cultural technologies of cleaning with smoke, eggs, salt, vinegar, flowers, herbs, bells, fire, water, and crystals.

I recommend figuring out some minimal strategies that can be worked into your day easefully and treating them as nonnegotiable to you. As always, we're not being perfectionists, we're being effective. You can always build on the minimum, and get fancy with it if you want, but make the smaller commitment first. You may find that a quick routine isn't enough for you, and choose to build more extensive fortification if you are especially empathic. Pay attention to and understand your particular sensitivities and the way your brain works. A dear friend of mine absolutely has to meditate twice a day to maintain her mental health. You will figure out what you need, but the first step is to take it seriously and try to develop a discipline.

FOR YOUR BODY: Make a boundaries and protection check part of getting ready for the day or leaving the house. In the same way you might check your makeup, hair, or clothes before you see other people, check to make sure you are protected. This may look like putting a crystal (I love black tourmaline or smoky quartz for this) in your bra or pocket, wearing an amulet underneath your clothes or jewelry set with shielding stones or charms (I'm partial to an evil eye charm), spritzing yourself with a protective spray, or strategically placing oil on your body to create a shield.

Remember that your skin is an important boundary between you and the world, so bring an element of protection and energetic clearing into your skin-care routine. There are so many beautiful products available that incorporate the powers of gem essences and herbs, handcrafted by independent herbalists and estheticians. Your basic body wash, scrub, and anointment (whether it be enchanted oils or Lubriderm) can easily be an energetic cleansing and protective practice. Remember, we're backed by the power of intention.

You can also engage specific spiritual bathing techniques. Seek spiritual bathing technologies from your ancestral lineages, such as the Hebrew tradition of mikveh, Germanic tradition of a beer and salt bath, Curanderismo tradition of limpias, and Hoodoo spiritual baths. I soak my hands in saltwater to extract energy that I run through my hands, arms, and heart center.

FOR YOUR ENERGY FIELD: A quick protection and grounding meditation will help you make sure your energies are where you want them before you engage with others. The back of your neck is a very sensitive psychic portal, so envision that there's a door there, and you are closing it tightly before leaving the house, and then cover it with anointing oil for an added seal. This will reduce the amount of psychic communication you engage in when you're out and about in the world at large. Try an aura cleansing and protection meditation.

FOR YOUR HOME: Clearing and protection in the home may look like energetic housekeeping: removing shoes at the door, burning herbs to clear the air in your home, spiritual sweeping, and floor washes. Give your house a blessing or hire a clergyperson to offer one. Protective spells for your space can be created through drawing sigils or placing amulets in your windows and doors, or painting hex signs like the Pennsylvania Dutch. Take up your space fully. Honor your space through regular cleaning and maintain a positive, peaceful, and beautiful ambience. Clutter can hold stagnant and outdated energies. Tending to and honoring your space is deep hearth magic.

AFFIRMATIONS AND GOALS

Affirmations are the cousin of intentions. They are little bursts of aligned energy that we use to propel ourselves in the direction we have set with our intention. Affirmations support and cheer us on to keep us headed toward our intention. When we write one, we are affirming ourselves; we are offering gentleness and positivity to ourselves. There is enough truly horrifying social and cultural messaging out there—our souls need some sweetness, and affirmations are a form of giving that loving-kindness to ourselves. This is a powerful offering of self-love as we shift away from self-soothing through consumption and into giving ourselves the emotional encouragement and attention we really need. Give these positive statements to yourself as a gift. We show that we care about the success and healing of others by remembering what they are trying to accomplish and cheering them on toward their goals. We do this for ourselves through affirmations, goals, and intentions.

Affirmations create new thought patterns in our minds and intro-duce positive and gentle voices to our inner landscape, which is prone to negative self-talk or punishing inner critics. As we introduce these voices regularly and consistently, we create new habits of mind and new patterns of thought. Essentially, we introduce a dissenting opinion to the tyranny of negative self-talk.

Also in the family are goals, which are specific achievements you plan to attain in the future. Goals are concrete and actionable, whereas an intention is a direction you are traveling. Think of intentions as more cosmic, deep-time, and evolutionary objectives, while goals are "specific, measurable, attainable, relevant, and time-bound" (or SMART, to refer-ence the common mnemonic for setting objectives). Your process toward your intention may have many phases of goal setting and accomplish-ment within it. Goals are an important part of taking action on your intentions, and will reappear in step 7.

HOW TO WRITE
AN INTENTION

Remember, you do not need to become a Pulitzer Prize–winning intention writer in order to get magic happening in your life. What makes your intention powerful is the energy you put into it and the devotion you invest in making it come true. Your heart makes it happen. The "grand dame of science fiction" and visionary Afrofuturist Octavia Butler regularly wrote in her personal journals lists of the accomplishments she intended on making true, adding after each intention, "So be it! See to it!" Multidisciplinary artist and healer Erykah Badu tells us, "Write it down on real paper with a real pencil with real intent and watch it get real. Spelling is a Spell." If high priestesses Erykah Badu and Octavia Butler tell us to do something, then we'd better take heed and get this skill set in our tool belt, and quickly. Using the power of our words to build worlds is the basis of all creation. We can speak, or in this case, write things into being.

There is no wrong way to write an intention, so defer to what feels personally right for you. There can be power in a statement of release: "I release spending that doesn't align with my priorities." Some schools of manifestation thought take the stance that intentions must stay positive and affirmative (reinforcing what you do want rather than what you don't want), in which case we might instead write, "I always spend in alignment with my highest priorities." When writing, claim your blessing in the present moment, for example: "I have stable and spacious housing" (rather than "I want to have stable and spacious housing"). And don't forget to bring gratitude to the mix: "I am grateful to have enough money to share with my friends."

Experienced manifesters know that getting something you asked for is only half the battle. Most of us have had the experience of getting something we wanted, only to find out it doesn't quite make us feel like we thought it would. When writing intentions, focus on how you want to feel rather than just a specific physical desire. This is another way we can subvert the consumerist cultures we've been raised in—rather than assuming a certain material thing will bring us joy, work on inviting joy itself and see what material blessings bring themselves to your doorstep as part of that process. The Universe has amazing ways of getting us the things we want and need, but getting what you want doesn't always come in the package you imagined it would. You might manifest a new boyfriend, only to realize that the relationship doesn't make you feel truly seen. If you focus rather on calling in a relationship that makes you feel truly seen, it may arrive in the form of a mentor or a friend, reducing the pressure you had previously felt to get that boyfriend.

Don't let this stop you from setting specific, tangible goals and working toward them. It may seem contradictory, but getting clear on exactly what you are trying to manifest is part of the process too. Like many of the realest things about life, it's a both/and. Get clear about what you want, but don't be so preoccupied by the specifics that you forget the bigger intentions behind it. Do the calculations to figure out that it's a $70,000 salary that's going to help you achieve your goal of living on your own, but don't forget to also focus your intentions on what that $70,000 represents to you: independence, sovereignty, being able to say yes to experiences you're excited about.

You might write:

I am being offered a new job that I love with a salary of over $70,000 a year, or something better to the highest good of all involved.

I am grateful to be experiencing joyful financial independence and sovereignty.

Getting specific, but allowing the Universe to surprise you, helps the vision be flexible in service of your larger goals. And, as each passing year reminds us, flexibility is absolutely key to helping us navigate this Earth journey. Adding "or to the greatest good of all involved" to our intentions and prayers is a lovely way of remembering that we don't always have all the information needed to solo plan our path. Intention allows us to cocreate with the Universe, our ancient elder ancestors, and our Spirit guides when we begin to undertake an endeavor or make a move. We open to the wisdom of those who hold the ancient, futuristic, wide-lens angle, and who may know more wisely what we need and how to get it.

It's OK if you encounter internal resistance or negative thoughts when you start writing intentions. Don't beat yourself up about it. Meet yourself where you are and make the process of intention and affirmation accessible for you. If something you want feels out of reach, and it's hard for you to believe that it could come true, I find using curiosity can open a window to the possibility. Framing your intention as a wonder is a step toward making big ideas accessible to you. In this style of intention, you would start by writing, "I wonder how I will [insert desire here]." For example, if flat-out stating "I make more than $100,000 per year" or "I am thankful to make over $100,000 per year" makes your inner critic go wild, start with "I wonder how I will make more than $100,000 per year." This allows you to play with the idea, and that playfulness is an opening to your creative power.

JOURNAL PROMPT
Make a Wish on the New Moon

Each moonth (you see what we did there?) offers a potent window of time to plant seeds and start something new. Use the day after the New Moon to handwrite your list of intentions. Writing by hand connects your body's own energetic force to the list.

Astrologer Jan Spiller advises, "It is vital to wait until after the exact time of the monthly New Moon before making wishes." She explains that it is best to set your intentions within eight hours of a New Moon, but setting them the day after is better than setting them even a few minutes before the New Moon.

ACTIVATE YOUR SUPPORT SYSTEM

Once you've got your intentions written down, and you're clear on
what you'd like to call forth into the material realm, invite your support
system to help you. This means letting your human inner circle—the
friends, family, comrades, and colleagues who cheer you on and lift you
up—in on your intentions. If there's no one around you who feels like
a safe and supportive listener, feel free to announce your goals to your
ancestors, your plants, or the ocean, or whisper it to a flower on your
daily walk. Declare it to the Universe or your deity of choice. Ask for
the support of the spirit world by declaring your intention ritualistically
at the New Moon. Activate the vibration of your intention by being
in engaged relationship with it and making it a part of your daily life.
Spread it through your conversations. Allow people and experiences that
resonate on your desired frequency to start coming to you. Embrace the
synchronicities that whisper to you that you're on the right track.

Some cultural traditions keep goals and accomplishments quiet to
protect from the evil eye, and if it is your practice to do so, focusing
on cultivating a private sphere of intention is extra important. Double
up on journaling, altar work, prayer, and meditating to the vibration
of your intention.

Your intentions should live in a place of honor in your life, like a guiding light. You might write them on a card and place it on your altar or in
your wallet, or tape it on your mirror. Go all *Being Mary Jane* and write
up a wall of sticky notes with your goals, intentions, and affirmations.
Paint it on paper and put it on the fridge. Make a collage vision board
about it. Whatever feels generative and significant to you. The important thing is to honor, appreciate, and support your intention, while also
being in an active relationship with it.

MAKE AN OFFERING

When we are making big asks of the Universe, and centering our own success, it is important to bring balance by also giving back. One of the greatest ways we can interrupt the mindset of capitalist colonialism is to stay centered in gratitude and right relationship. So-called Western culture tells us to extract what we want or need at any cost. This causes us to view exploitation and one-sided relationships as normal, when they are actually deeply unnatural. We easily slip into exploitative treatment toward both others and ourselves. Internalized exploitation culture can look like scarcity mindset, obsession with productivity, prioritizing results over relationship, and neglecting rest, care, and reflection. If we don't check the ways that we have internalized the exploitative nature of capitalism, we can bring those attitudes to our spiritual life and our healing process.

All relationships are multisided. That includes your relationships with both the spiritual world and the larger human community. Kyriarchy permits and normalizes the illusion of one-sided relationships, where what only one person wants matters—the boss, the individual, the stockholder. We can resist that untruth by tapping into and being responsible to the interconnected web of life of which we are all a part. Interconnection, which eschews both disconnection and codependency, is the natural way of existence. Recognizing and embracing interconnection means we are aligning with truth.

While the work of healing our personal finances is an important contribution to collective healing, this process does not happen in isolation or in a vacuum. It happens in relationship to all other humans, to our societal structures, to the spirit world, and to the Earth itself. So what does it look like to show respect and care in those relationships as we get our finances right? Making offerings, being grateful, and opening to guidance from wisdom sources greater than ourselves. Making an offering as a primary element of posing a request teaches us so much and allows us to unlearn extractive ways of being. Making offerings may be a

AFFIRMATION

I invest
my energy,
time, effort, and
resources in
intentional
ways.

new concept to you, but don't let it feel confusing. It is our natural state to be connected rather than transactional. Giving back is a profound way to say thank you for what you already have.

If you want the spiritual world to show up for you, invite it into your life and offer hospitality and reciprocity, just as you would in a human relationship. Each different ancestral lineage has its own spin on the details, but the basic idea is to offer little gifts of attention, energy, or material resources as part of building and strengthening spiritual relationships. This can look like lighting a candle or burning incense, placing a glass of water or flowers on your altar, or offering a portion of food or beverage. Outside it can look like asking permission and offering back a song or a prayer when you pick an herb or a flower or planting a new plant in your yard for the Earth spirits. Speak a little prayer, anything that comes to your mind. You can greet the spirits and let them know the offering is dedicated to them. Once you get in the practice, make offerings to the spirits of the land that you live on, your ancestors, the collective elder spirits, and any particular deities that you individually work with.

JOURNAL PROMPT
An Attitude of Gratitude

Write down ten things you are grateful for today.

Extra credit: If you want to extend this to developing a daily practice, take a small notebook or use an app on your phone to list ten things you are grateful for each day. This practice can help with depression and hopelessness as well as help you notice the improvements on your goals as you move along your process.

If you're not as comfortable with the spiritual angle, remember that making an offering can be practical and material as well. Reparations and resource return, what we call tzedakah in Judaism, is ancestral healing. Reparations are both part of a process of apology and the return of resources that were stolen and extracted. Turning toward these practices isn't radical, just rational and respectful. This is an acknowledgment that right and easeful relationship requires reciprocity, and an acknowledgment that the human relationship to reciprocity has been deeply warped over the last five hundred years. Maybe your role in reparations is receiving. This is not a tit-for-tat reciprocity, but an acknowledgment of giving and receiving that is based in an alignment with divine truth. Offering money, resources, time, labor, and access to both people who are experiencing more oppression than you and to the living human descendants of the traditional stewards of the land that you live on is a nonnegotiable part of being in right relationship with money. If you are reading this book, you are experiencing some sort of relative privilege, so stretch to understand where your role is to give and where your role is to receive. This is a process of human repair and healing.

RITUAL

Say a Little Prayer

This may seem so basic, but lots of people don't feel comfortable praying. You might be one of them. You may feel like you don't know how or unsure if you're "doing it right." You may try to pray and never feel like your prayers are "going" anywhere, not connecting to a Spirit source. Prayer just means talking to Spirit, and may be done out loud or in your head. Pour your heart out—your worries, your dreams, your hopes, and your intentions. Prayer can take place anywhere at any time and will always be heard, received, and held.

It can feel special to pray in a sacred place, and you have the power to create a temporary temple for yourself. Cover your head with a large scarf, shawl, or piece of fabric when you pray and close the front in order to create a private space for you to be intimate with the Divine. This also serves to both protect your psychic space and concentrate your own energy field in order to direct it powerfully in prayerful intention. Some people find going out into nature helpful in feeling connected and intimate enough with Spirit to have a conversation.

Incorporate a special or regular time to pray. This could be weekly at a place of worship or daily upon waking. I pray before bed and in the shower. Notice the tiny miracles of the day and say a prayer of thanks.

STEP

5

Owning the Obstacles

Explore an array of insights on common emotional and spiritual financial blocks.

MONEY MAGIC ALLIES

Astrological Role Model

Gemini: Gemini draws power from being open to allll the ideas. They want to see every possible perspective and they are excited to process knowledge. Geminis know that they can overcome any obstacle if only they get the right information to outsmart the situation. They're rarely intimidated by a challenge because every challenge has an embedded adventure. Exploring the territory is what makes it fun.

Crystal Friends

Rose Quartz: This pink stone encourages you to open up to the process and the possibilities contained within it, while supporting your heart and emotions with gentleness through the inevitable rough patches. Rose quartz encourages you to trust and love yourself enough to release your grip on the old and know that you will make it through to something better.

Malachite: This beautiful green stone activates a different part of your heart: its bravery. It imbues you with the fortitude and courage to transform any fears or doubts, especially with regard to money. The swirling and complex patterns on the surface of a polished malachite remind you that the twists and turns of your journey are what make it, and you, beautiful.

Tiny Tarot Reading

Justice and The Hierophant: These cards are bringing you the message that now is the time to pause, gather information, and weigh what's at hand before taking action. The Hierophant wants to educate you, imparting a deeper wisdom and philosophy, one that explores what and how you have been taught. It is both the experiences you've had and also the meanings you have assigned to those experiences that really form your personal worldview. It may be time to do some renovations on your stance, releasing the points of view that no longer help you grow and upgrading how you assign meaning to parts of your experience. Think of it like a spiritual windshield washing. Sitting with the information and sifting through it will help you see which parts have become tarnished or stagnant.

It is only you who knows where you have transgressed the boundaries of your own self-interest and only you who can hold yourself fully accountable for learning to do different. Peer through the outer layers of your behaviors to perceive your real motivations and be accountable to that truth. You don't have to justify your actions to anyone but yourself, so make sure you feel really good and in integrity about how you are acting. What do you need to learn in order to act in greater alignment with your own health? The laws of cause and effect are activated at this time. When you understand your behavior, you can change your behavior. When you change your behavior, you change the course of your life and the human story forever. You will do better as you know better.

Cup of Tea

Rose, linden, and elderflower will bring peaceful self-acceptance and feelings of being seen.

OK, so we've figured out our starting point, planned our destination, and gotten our butt in gear headed out the door. But if getting from point A to point B was as easy as that, we would've already been there. There are plenty of obstacles on the road ahead. Clearly identifying them is a huge and necessary step to overcoming them. How will we know which tool to pull out of our backpack if we haven't pinpointed our challenge?

As intense as it can be to come face-to-face with our own unique pantheon of issues, knowing is always better than not knowing. Having your back to something is the most dangerous position you can stand in. Facing these issues head-on means they don't come for you, you call for them. They won't blindside you anymore or creep up when you are least prepared. We've worked really hard during this whole process and laid all the groundwork we need to be prepared for this. You have completely got this.

Because the idea of emotional healing is somewhat taboo, we don't always acknowledge the extent to which our emotional wounds impact our financial lives. But this is the key to unlocking so much more success for yourself. You must address these issues and clearly see these qualities in yourself, and then you can start coming in to right relationship with money. Having the right language can help.

Language and literacy are gifts of empowerment. This is a literacy of your financial self, building off the work you did in step 2. Think of it as the next level, getting language for parts of your financial self you may have noticed but did not have the words to describe. Being open to this deeper layer of knowledge of financial self is going to open doors for you. You are about to become unstoppable.

This step is all about identifying the blocks on your path to financial success. Our goal is to see what is getting in our way emotionally, logistically, and energetically so that we can bust those walls down intelligently with the right tool for the job.

STOP MINIMIZING
YOUR FEELINGS

Naming, validating, and transmuting our internal blocks is the key to financial liberation. We're accustomed to being gaslit around our financial management. If we would just try harder and not be so irresponsible, everything would be fine. It's easy to feel bad about ourselves when we try to do something like budget over and over and fail repeatedly. It's especially easy to feel bad when we act as though all the traumas and frustrations that are activated when we attempt to "adult" aren't real. We're never taught that feelings are a part of finance. Stop trying to force your way into financial success. Trying the same solution that didn't work the last three times is not going to fix the problem. Work smarter, not harder, by taking the time to see what the real problem is.

Our interior life matters so much. But since it can't be seen by others, and can only be perceived, not seen, by even ourselves, it's easy to disregard or deprioritize it, especially when trying to focus on practical matters like money. We can't talk about money without talking about the activations that occur along with it, and the friction points that occur between what gets activated and what we're "supposed" to be able to do. Money, like most anything in life, is a multidimensional experience, and we lie to ourselves when we don't one hundred percent validate that truth.

Be gentle with yourself as you do this work. So many people ignore this level of self-awareness and healing. I think you're awesome and brave for being here and I'm proud of you.

MINDFULNESS MOMENT

Embody Growth

Before we dive in, take a minute to center in a calm, resilient energy. Sit comfortably with your feet on the floor if you're able, take a deep breath, and exhale loudly, letting go of some of the stress and tension you may have felt picking up a book about money. Take another deep breath and envision yourself as fertile, rich, dark soil. Allow yourself to be receptive to unfolding growth and unfurling transformation. Get excited about all the seeds of awareness, knowledge, and maturation we are about to plant together. Admire your own potential for change. Exhale any pressure you feel to grow into anything other than your truest, most actualized self. Take another deep breath and appreciate the beautiful flourishing that is about to occur in your money garden. Give thanks for the rain and the sun, as both will help you reach your goals. Embrace the abundance of the future. Embody growth.

PRESENTING...
THE BLOCKS!

We're going to name these blocks not only because we plan on facing them but also because getting the language for what we are experiencing is a form of healing. Believing the emotional dimension of your finances is real, and having the words to name it is a fundamental step on the healing process.

Not every described "block" will resonate with you. Keep an eye out and notice where you see yourself and your own behavior or feelings reflected on the page. If you read something that resonates for you, take a moment to write it down in your journal or highlight it in your book. This will be a place you can return to and dig deeper into on your healing journey. Also, Lord knows human life is complex and this list is in no way complete. There are definitely parts of your financial experience you may not see named here. Use this journey of exploration to allow some of that personal knowledge to loosen up and flow through. Write your ideas in the margins or in your journal.

Feel free to step away from the page and cry, breathe, walk, take a shower, do a dance video. Don't forget to hydrate, eat, stretch, and nourish yourself. Every hero's journey has obstacles, and it is in facing them that we gain greater insight into our unique purpose and path, become initiated into our personal power, and receive the reward of transformation.

Avoidance

Avoidance is by far one of the most common money blocks! It's easy to feel like we're doing ourselves a favor by avoiding things. It seems like it will save you from stress and overwhelm, but it's actually disempowering, creates deep subconscious stress, and is bad for your self-esteem. Witnessing yourself repeatedly not handling your business is terrible for your self-image. We must give ourselves tons of compassion for how we became who we are, but compassion and enabling are two different things.

Avoidance can arise when moving from the familiar to the unfamiliar. If money management feels new to you, and you weren't given adequate or resonant role models for financial success, then this world can activate overwhelm, alienation, and shame. And it's a quick trip from there to denial and avoidance. Super normal, truly. Facing money may activate resentment and grief about the financial education and parenting you didn't get and the factors that contributed to that. Notice these feelings as they arise and validate them. Give yourself a vote of confidence that says you are resilient enough to weather those passing feelings in the interest of becoming financially healthy. It's understandable to want to avoid the areas of your life where you feel disempowered or incompetent. It can be especially tempting to put off your finances if you are a strong, successful person who has plenty of other consuming and exciting things to focus on, such as parenting, networking, making art, or participating in your spiritual community.

You can do this, and the truth of the matter is that you cannot get out of handling your finances. No matter how many times you look away, that tax return, that overspending habit, that unpaid bill will be right there in the background, creating a cycle of cause and effect that deeply impacts every moment of your experience. Get in there and put your hands on your financial life. Take control of the landscape. Face it and them. Avoidance cultivates crisis, and you are done cultivating crisis for yourself.

Family Baggage

When you are exploring your family money story, make sure to go back to generations before your parents or grandparents. Having a grasp on the experiences of your ancestors can make the money habits we have make all the sense in the world. You might find it hard to understand why your middle-class mother hoarded groceries while living an almost infinitely resourced suburban existence, but understanding that her great-great-grandmother lost a child during a famine can help connect the dots.

Familial money baggage gets passed down through epigenetics and household habits, and you are probably schlepping some. It is delicate and painful work, but making space to sit with the legacy of trauma in your family line and the way it specifically intersects with money will provide you with a lot of context for your financial healing journey. Experiences of trauma also heavily impact family issues that are adjacent to money but aren't always validated as impacting your finances: Addiction, divorce, division of labor, access to privacy, and family members' capacity for intimacy all impact our experience of money growing up.

As you notice how some of these habits of mind and habits of behavior have trickled down to the way you manage money, commit to making active choices rather than passively re-creating patterns. Nothing that happened to you as a child or in your family home is your fault. But now as an adult, you get to choose. And if you keep choosing things that disempower you, that's an important place to explore. It can sometimes feel like a betrayal to your family to make more (or less) money than them or to change class status, even if they encouraged you to do so. It's time to shred any invisible contracts you have with your family that keep you stuck and disempowered financially and perpetuate stagnation in the lineage. Remember that you are also an ancestor in the making and do it for the lineage of the future.

Boredom

It is definitely true that the day-to-day tasks of financial healing often qualify for the #boringselfcare category. Even worse are the parts of the job that feel both challenging *and* boring. I understand that it can be hard to get it up for this work when there are so many more compelling parts of your day. Taxes, budgeting, and life insurance can linger on the bottom of the to-do list because they are just plain not fun. While it may seem silly, or easy to beat yourself up about, notice when you're avoiding your finances because they seem just plain boring, and try to zhuzh up your process. Get super cute office supplies and a file box. Start a money book club with a friend. Find a hot financial coach. Just make it happen. Handling your biz does not have to be dry and uninspiring.

Scarcity

My favorite book on the subject of scarcity is Victoria Castle's *The Trance of Scarcity*, and in it she lays out a definition of the term that has been my go-to ever since. Scarcity is the belief or sensation that "there is not enough," "I am not enough," or "nice things are for other people, but not for me." For example, "I'd love to own a house, but I know I'll never be able to."

Feeling paralyzed by small spending decisions, an inability to allow yourself to buy the basics for yourself, such as new socks and undies, always feeling like the other shoe is going to drop, or feeling like the good money you just made is sure to be your last are all signs of scarcity mentality.

The antidote to scarcity mindset is cultivating an attitude of abundance, which says, "There is enough and I am deserving."

Shock

Shock is a trauma response that your nervous system activates when you experience something too negatively overwhelming to process. It is part of the fight, flight, freeze, fawn response system categorized by therapists and researchers who study complex trauma and the way it lives in our bodies. The automatic, involuntary freeze response is triggered by your parasympathetic nervous system. This part of your system wants to bring you down to calm by any means necessary and will go to great lengths to get you there. When you are in shock, it is because your body has made a split-second decision that the best way to survive the experience you are having is to shut down your ability to feel. My therapist told me it's so it won't hurt so bad when the lion eats you. The problem with shock is that it can linger and leave you with a long-term incapacity to feel or understand your feelings about a difficult situation. Your feelings themselves are seen as a threat and so your system subconsciously represses them. If you are not able to access your feelings about difficult things that have occurred in your life, especially those that relate to your financial habits, you won't be able to work through them and get to the other side. This could be a divorce, a childhood incident, getting fired, or being shamed for your desires. Shock can occur in any situation that overwhelms us to a high enough level. If this resonates with you, talk to a therapist or access some online education about how to move through and out of freeze mode.

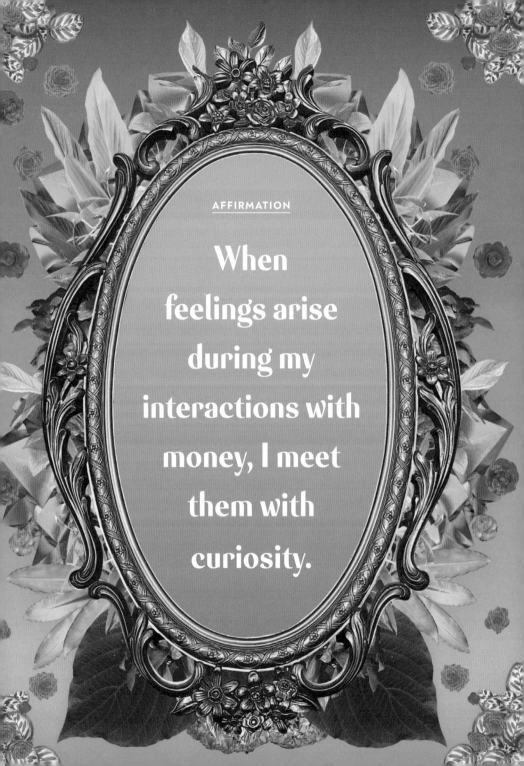

AFFIRMATION

When feelings arise during my interactions with money, I meet them with curiosity.

Anger

Anger is a signal that something is wrong, and your anger and rage are important and valid. I'm not saying it's easy (or culturally supported), but you have got to make space and time to feel, release, and move with and through your anger. This is even harder if you are living in a body that is societally stereotyped as angry, threatening, and/or intimidating. Rage is a valid and sane emotion, and many of the things we feel it toward are present in our finances. Anger at institutions, family members, coworkers, and yourself can build into a simmering rage that is always threatening to overflow. When it doesn't have a release valve, you wind up dealing with the spillage when you are overwhelmed, upset, and not in control of the experience. You can cause harm to yourself and your relationships, not to mention your finances. Making space to feel, validate, and process anger will help you make peaceful, grounded decisions in the rest of your life.

Unprocessed Grief

Unhealed grief clogs your system and leaves you stagnant and suffering. Loss and disappointment are often intertwined with negatively impactful financial experiences. We may need to make space to grieve the material care we should have received as a child but didn't get, we may need to grieve the impact of violence on our ancestral financial lineage, we may need to grieve a moment in our life when we lost someone who supported us both emotionally and materially. We may need to grieve the loss of stability, a career, or an opportunity, such as a scholarship or an important client. Going deep and fully experiencing our sadness and disappointment is essential work. And again, the only way to move past a feeling is to fully experience it. You can't bypass your healing process. You have to get deeply sad so that you aren't haunted by constant low-level sadness. You have to let go of the thing you lost.

My quick and dirty recipe for processing grief is this: Carve out a substantial piece of time—a whole day or several hours at least. It helps to make space somewhat regularly, or more than once. Divide your time into four equal parts and spend one on each of the following steps: fully feeling the loss, releasing and letting go, comforting yourself or being comforted, and resting from your hard work. This may look like spending an hour remembering the thing you lost and thinking about the hurt you have experienced, then an hour writing about your feelings and burning the paper, then an hour wrapped in a big cozy blanket speaking gently in an affirming way to yourself, and then an hour watching TV or sleeping. And always and forever, don't forget to breathe, hydrate, and eat snacks.

New Money

When you catch your first big financial break, whether it be the highest salary you've ever made or a big account or high-earning year in your business, there is obviously a wave of elation. When the financial dust settles, the joy is often followed by a wave of thoughts like "I made more money this year than I've ever made in my life, so where the fuck did it all go?" There are a few things that are common at this stage that will answer that big question for you. First, when you have spent years struggling with scarcity, suddenly being able to buy things is a huge lifestyle shift. It's easy to experience a pendulum swing into buying whatever you want whenever you want, and that gets expensive. In time, your finances usually achieve equilibrium, but becoming aware of your new spending behaviors may mean it's time to work toward that balance. Second is what I call the deferred maintenance of your life. Deferred maintenance is a real estate term that refers to postponing repairs. If you've been broke forever, you landed at this higher-level income with some serious delayed expenses. Finally being able to pay for new glasses, dental work, furniture, and car repairs is a massive blessing but will eat up that check real quick—exponentially so if you're paying for the deferred needs of family members as well. The third, simple as it is, is that people who are under-earning accumulate debt, and whether you paid it off in a big lump or you have large monthly debt payments, filling in the hole can easily chip away at a new paycheck. The important thing to remember is not to lose the hope and joy of achieving stability for yourself. Your higher earning is a major accomplishment. Stay mindful of where your money is going and grateful for the level up, and you will soon achieve the balance you need and be able to start building for the future.

JOURNAL PROMPT

The First Time

When did you get your first paycheck and how did it feel? How much was it? What did you do with it?

Privilege, Oppression, and Theft

Privilege simply means a lack of oppression because of a certain identity marker. As we talked about in step 1, understanding the idea of intersectional identity is key to understanding where you experience privilege. Look at each piece of your identity and ask, "Am I experiencing systemic hardship and oppression because I am _____?" For example, am I experiencing oppression because I am a woman? Yes. Am I experiencing systemic hardship because I am white? No. Am I experiencing random hardship in my life at the hands of fate? Yes. Does that mean I'm not privileged? No. People who are living in multiply marginalized bodies are going to deal, systemically, with more violence and fewer resources.

OK, now we're on the same page. Privilege has a massive impact on people's finances because almost all the systemic oppression that has been implemented throughout time has been though economic and financial means. So wherever you are in the intersecting web, your money situation has been and is impacted daily by the hierarchical power structure of our globalized economy. Oppression primarily operates via theft—theft of land, labor, lives, language, lineage, self-concept, self-determination, ownership, and stewardship of resources. No matter where you're coming from, you have either stolen or been stolen from, and many, many people have occupied both roles. Really being present with that truth is overwhelming to reconcile, to say the least, which is why it has been largely obscured by those who have even a small amount of economic power or advantage. The second layer to that reality is that almost all of us are trapped in a system where we are ongoingly both implicated in extracting from other humans and the Earth and exploited to the point of exhaustion at every turn. As a fact, it is a lot to hold.

To be on one hand vehemently opposed to exploitation and on the other hand engaging it with every purchase you make is a double bind, and it is emotionally distressing. As I said back in step 1, sanity is going to require that you accept that these realities may not be able to be reconciled. Some of us spend a tremendous amount of energy trying to make life make sense, and sometimes we have to accept that multiple irreconcilable things may be true at the same time.

When you subconsciously demand that your financial choices live in a reconciled place you will inevitably be blocked by impossibility, which causes suffering, decision fatigue, and inaction. This can look like obsessing over the environmental and social cost of every product at the grocery store and ending up leaving overwhelmed and depressed. It's a reasonable response, but it's not viable given that you have to do it once a week for the rest of your life. It will keep you feeling trapped. A scaled-up example of this may be keeping a large amount of money, perhaps an inheritance, in your savings account for an extended period of time, frozen and unable to make a decision about where or whether to invest it. Trying to make a nonexploitative plan to invest inherited hoarded wealth within a capitalist system is just straight up not going to happen.

So what to do? Since we can't be ethical, we're going to strive for responsible. Since we can't eliminate harm, we're going to embrace paths of harm reduction. Most of all, we're going to be honest. Living in self-perpetuated poverty is not reparative. Present-time economic and earning status is one of the only privileges that can be actively given up, and I see a lot of "radical" white people specifically attempt to cross this privileged status off their identity markers. This is performative poverty that has nothing in common with the real experience of being unable to access the opportunity to make enough money to survive and even less in common with managing the impact of generational lack of resources on your psyche and reality. Part of the motivation to do this is a genuine desire to relate to people who are struggling, but another part is to not have to take responsibility. And ultimately, it's a self-serving action that alleviates your guilt but causes no real positive economic impact.

Tempting tactics that are actually harmful include but are not limited to: ignoring, minimizing, invalidating, or invisibilizing the truth and our role in it. So that means facing finances head-on. Handling your money badly does not exonerate you from financial privilege. Ignoring your finances and shying away from responsibility for your financial health does not change the truth of your position within the economic hierarchy. You had no personal control over where you landed in this human story, but you are responsible for managing what you have been handed. Privilege breeds fragility, and the antidote is resilience and responsibility. Financially, this means getting comfortable talking about and understanding money. It means knowing what you have and what your parents' situation is. It means being able to discuss numbers openly— salary, savings, price tags. It means understanding how much things cost and having literacy about how money works—credit scores, car and house loans, retirement savings, interest rates. It means knowing where your money is and what it's doing. What is your 401(k) invested in? You get there by learning and doing it enough times that you push through the discomfort and find that it lessens. It means that discomfort is not a reason to not do something. Build your capacity to believe, sit with, talk about, and act on hard truths. Moving toward liberation is an honor.

Fear of Selling Out and Glorification of the Struggle

If you have spent time in activist spaces or subcultural artistic scenes, or anywhere that economic struggle is seen as miserable but saintly, you may grapple with rising desires for financial stability as you age. I call this post-punk baggage. There are two main blocks under this umbrella. The first is fear about other people's opinion of you.

Most people I talk to who are afraid of "selling out" are mainly afraid of what other people think of them, and how their image will change if they are perceived as caring about money or making money. Usually these folks have decided and reconciled for themselves that they are done struggling and ready for more stability and income. They feel clear and grounded in that desire. But there is a huge fear of being perceived as not caring about community politics or accessibility, as well as a fear of losing intimacy and connection with people they care about. Engage transparency and dialogue in order to get ahead of the conversation you fear will tear you down.

There are some hard truths here, and one of them is that, while it certainly doesn't have to, most times becoming more successful does involve some loss of relationships. There are people who will not be able to go with you to the places you want to go, and not through your own choice. Make sure that you are acting in alignment with your values and take your politics with you. Success and money don't change who you are, but they do reveal who you are. You can't control whether people like or respect you; you have to live your life so that you like and respect yourself. If you have relationships that are built on unclear perceptions of each other, then it's time to release them. It is one of my absolute least favorite parts of life that sometimes people have to part ways, but it is a deeply true one. There are also just flat-out haters, whether they be family or community members or so-called friends, whose own insecurities and jealousy will not allow them to walk with you in success and stability. They may feel judged and implicated by your accomplishments, confronted by what they themselves want but have not yet achieved. It's always relevant to note that a lot of people who are slinging judgment in the court of public opinion about how others are money-grubbing capitalists are not being transparent about their own finances. Just because it is a subcultural perception that the "artist class" is an economic class, it's not really, and there are plenty of people flagging poverty that actually have access to wealth, family networks of resource to fall back on, or partners or high-paying day jobs that are enabling their participation. Only you know the circumstances of where you're coming from.

The second block in this category is the fear of your perception of yourself. The real issue is that with cash flow comes responsibility. Not only is there the learning curve of how to steward your resources, but also all kinds of existential quandaries arise that make you face your values in ways that are uncomfortable. It's easy to think that if you got more money, you would do this or never do that. It's another thing to have to confront that experience as a reality and see how you feel. If you suddenly got an inheritance, would you actually give it reparatively, or would you want to keep it to do something for yourself? If you got a high-paying job, would you recognize the element of privilege in it (if you have race or gender privilege, for example) or would you want to believe the success came completely on your own merits? Making money is a test of your values. The fear of becoming wealthy or well-resourced is not a fear of money; it's really a fear about your own lack of integrity. But your integrity is not based in struggle. You can take your integrity with you into the experience of being more heavily resourced.

Perfectionism, Expansiveness, and Getting Lost in the Details

Perfectionists often struggle with their finances. If you alternate between hyper-organizing every last detail and then avoidance, this one's for you. Doing projects so extensively that they become huge and Herculean tasks results in overwhelm, shutdown, or just plain lack of enough time or resources to execute. I see this with tax clients who document their expenses and income down to a level of detail that is unnecessary for me as the accountant and exceeds their information needs. This may seem like a neutral or even positive trait, but it often results in filing late or accumulating years of unfiled back taxes. Learning to discern which details are important can be more or less challenging depending on your neuro reality, but spending consistent time with your finances and noticing the moment of shutdown will strengthen the muscle and build awareness of the pattern.

When I was a teenager, I would procrastinate on all my school projects till the last minute, and then strive to complete them in a way that was very detail oriented and truly engaging and interesting to me. I almost never got done on time and would end up with a half-finished but very high-concept project, getting a C or a D grade. Don't let perfect be the enemy of good. Done is better than perfect. If you often go big and then don't get it done, try to explore what it looks like to do the quick and dirty version of things.

Self-Sabotage and Addictive Behaviors

When you notice yourself acting in ways you know aren't good for you and you don't feel in control of whether you stop, that's an addiction red flag. When you engage these behaviors consciously or subconsciously in order to cause havoc or pain, or to punish yourself, that's self-sabotage. There are multiple addictions that surround money: shopping addiction, gambling addiction, workaholic tendencies, gifting addiction attached to codependency. It doesn't have to be extreme; almost everybody engages in some addictive behavior with money.

Financial reinforcement (such as receiving money or receiving material items through shopping) makes our brain feel like we're getting a reward. Our brain communicates this to us by releasing a little hit of a chemical called dopamine into our system, and it feels good as hell. So it's super easy to engage in addictive behaviors around money because it produces a high in our system.

On a chemical level, shopping registers for most of us as receiving something (the items we bought) rather than a loss of money. On a subconscious level, your brain does register that you're doing both, and if it isn't a wise choice for you, that's where the underlying shame spiral kicks in. Shame then contributes to the kind of secrecy and concealing that any other type of addictive behavior can elicit. This becomes most dangerous when you start investing in concealing truths from and deluding yourself. It's not uncommon to even go into a sort of blackout state and engage in online shopping. This is designed to get you the thing your system wants (the dopamine) while allowing you to disengage from any conflicting facts (such as not being able to afford what you bought).

Remember that most addictive habits are an attempt to get your needs met, so treat yourself with kindness while exploring this idea. Notice if there are certain experiences that start the chain reaction that ends in you engaging a destructive behavior. Do you online shop after you have a hard day at work, when you experience a microaggression, or when your best friend isn't available to talk? Pay attention to what your sweet self is telling you, and when that inner child needs to be comforted and held. Seeing the cycle is the first step, and disrupting the cycle is the second one. But remember, the disruption needs to offer a healthier alternative, not just shame and punishment. Telling yourself, "You're doing that bad thing again, cut it out!" is almost never an effective strategy. Try choosing an alternative that is more conducive to your financial health, such as saying, "No online shopping tonight, but let's take a bubble bath." Find the yes and give it to yourself.

JOURNAL PROMPT
High Life

Where do you experience a lack of control in your financial behavior, or feel like you can't stop yourself? How do you get a dopamine hit around money? Are there times when you seek this out even when you know it's not good for you or your financial health?

Self-Abuse and Negative Self-Talk

If you are mean to yourself when you try to manage your money, then no wonder you're avoiding it. Sometimes we don't like the things that happen inside our head when we approach finances. It might get loud or angry or even abusive in there.

My tax client Tabitha is a super-accomplished therapist who specializes in cultivating empathy in her clients. But when she works on her bookkeeping or budgeting, she talks to herself in what I began to dub the Mean Teacher voice. This voice would tell her she wasn't learning fast enough, she wasn't getting it right, she should have figured it out sooner—basically that her bookkeeping should have been handled already, and she's an asshole for waiting this long to figure it out. Who on Earth would want to do their bookkeeping if it meant they had to hang out with Mean Teacher? That person sucks.

Even worse, she didn't realize how hard this was on her, because she just thought these things were facts and therefore she deserved to have to be face-to-face with these hard truths. Because her inner self-loving force is smart and protective, it started pushing her to avoid the situation in order to avoid her own self-abuse.

That avoidance decreased her financial self-esteem, which made her feel like even more of a failure, which resulted in a downward spiral that made the mean voice sound even more valid.

Negative self-talk is just as inappropriate and hurtful as if an outside-your-head voice were talking to you like this. You wouldn't, as an adult, tolerate a teacher who spoke to you or your child like this, nor would you think this was a very effective teaching strategy. Fire your abusive inner "coach" ASAP and start writing a job description for the patient, encouraging, and effective economics teacher you really deserve.

Waiting to Be Saved, and Other Fairy-Tale Fantasies

Femmes especially can put high value on things that happen by chance, come by luck, or were earned through beauty. Although it can be tempting while in the throes of seemingly unfixable financial troubles to imagine someone swooping in and erasing your struggles, subconsciously banking on this as your backup plan can be a delusional vestige of childhood.

If you have repeatedly experienced being rescued from your financial mistakes in real life, by family members or partners, you may experience a lack of belief in your capacity to do it on your own. This impacts your self-esteem. This is not to invalidate real and healthy networks of support and mutual aid that lift up each according to their need, but rather a call to release unhealthy fantasies that stem from a lack of confidence in your own capacity.

Bad Investments

Guilt, shame, and regret about specific financial experiences from your past can stop you from moving on and making fresh, new moves. This can come up especially if debt or divorce is a part of your money story. You may feel angry about accumulated student loan debt from a degree you either didn't finish or don't use. You may know you got screwed over in your divorce settlement because you didn't have the resources or bandwidth to fight for what was fair. You might have fought and still got screwed. You may have taken out a credit card in your first semester of college, charged it up, and spent years and years paying it back and trying to repair your score. You may have helped your ex build a business and had to walk away with nothing. At the end of the day, you have to take ownership of your part in what happened and forgive yourself. What did you learn about how you'd like to move forward differently in the future?

It is OK to make a bad investment, whether you sunk money, time, emotions, effort, or all of the above. It's normal to feel embarrassed, ashamed, and angry, but you have to forgive yourself so that you can have closure. When we don't get closure on an issue, it haunts us. It's like walking around with an open wound, a pain that is so apparent and loud that it sucks up all the air. Learn from your mistakes, cut your losses, and move on. Everything you've been through makes you the complex and wise creature you are today. Arrive in current time and release the past. Don't schlep this resentment with you into the future.

Not Envisioning a Future

This is a heavy one, but many of us did not think we would make it to our thirties or forties. Not being able to conceptualize an adult or elder future for yourself due to addiction, suicidal ideation, mental health challenges, or physical health challenges can impact both your financial decisions and your capacity to conceptualize long-term planning, such as retirement. Experiencing domestic violence or living in fear of experiencing queer or transphobic violence can have the same effect. When you're in survival mode, just focusing on getting by day to day, it's hard to build for the future. I want to say a deep thank you to you for doing all the incredibly difficult work of staying alive to this moment, and for doing the work of healing into conceptualizing a thriving future for yourself. You are loved by me.

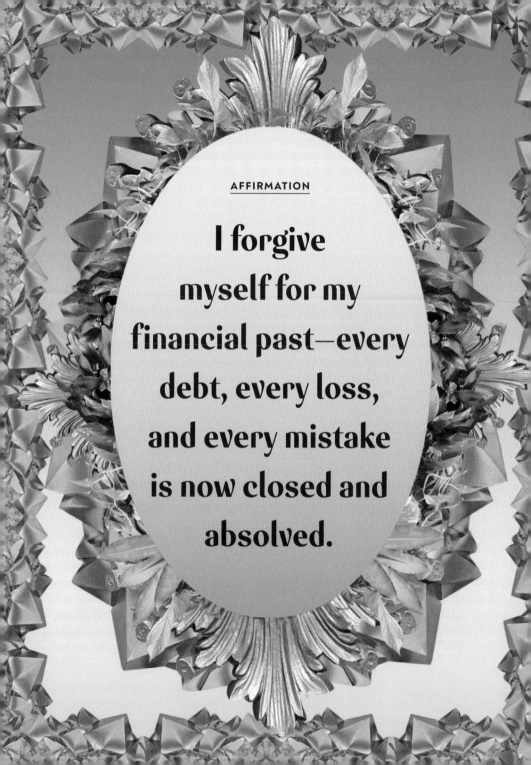

AFFIRMATION

I forgive myself for my financial past—every debt, every loss, and every mistake is now closed and absolved.

Resistance

Your resistance energy is sacred and very sane. It is needed by the larger human family. There is so much happening politically, socially, and environmentally that needs and deserves resistance. Fighting against the mainstream tide of gender roles, racialization, and hollow consumerism is important. It's also deeply exhausting. Because of the way that our finances are intertwined with the government (taxes) and institutional monoliths (banks, investing, education, and earning), it's easy to start feeling resentful and angry at them. Please do not waste your precious life force resisting your finances or your taxes. It is very painful that your material survival is grafted together with the very systems you intelligently seek to fight back against, but it is a fact. When you allow this aggression to harm your finances, you are doing much more damage to yourself than to the man. For example, filing your tax return late because you resent your tax dollars being spent on an obscenely large military budget does absolutely nothing to contribute to peace, and you actually end up paying more in the end due to penalties and interest.

Tolerating Bullshit Unnecessarily

Just because you can deal with something doesn't mean you have to. Sometimes we tolerate things just because we have the skill set to do so. We are used to having subpar things, so we keep a busted mattress even though we can afford to replace it. Navigating our narcissistic parents made us good at managing difficult people, so we stay at a job with an abusive boss rather than looking for a new situation. And sometimes we just get used to certain circumstances without remembering we have the agency to change them. What is not serving you? What do you need to let go of? What are you tolerating? What is complicating your life that you can release? What is causing you suffering or discomfort that you can stop allowing into your space? What decision could you make in the next twenty-four hours that would bring ease to your life? How much happier would you be?

Emotional Pain

What is the pain you are avoiding when you ignore your finances? Unexplored emotional territory is terrifying. We are afraid of and sometimes not ready for exploration and shift. When you interact with money, personal problems and traumas will rise to the surface to meet you. Some of them may be too overwhelming to wrestle with in the moment, but acknowledge them. New layers will reveal themselves to you and come to the surface when they are ready to be healed, when you are able to transmute them. It is an honor and a reflection of your maturity and capacity when a trauma presents itself to you. It means you have grown wise and stable enough to face the truth and metabolize it.

MINDFULNESS MOMENT

Feel the Burn

When you feel emotional pain arising, try to be curious about the sensation and track it. Allow yourself to notice exactly where in your body the feeling resides and what it feels like. Follow the feeling as it moves around in your body. Does it feel tight, scratchy, gripping, floaty, contracted? Does it feel hot or cold?

Financial Codependency

Codependency may manifest as protecting people from the natural consequences of their actions, believing people owe you because of what you have given them, or being overgenerous because you want to be liked. It can also cause you to be extremely loyal and stay in financially harmful relationships for too long. Signs of financial codependency can look

like a lack of boundaries, such as buying gifts you can't afford, supporting family members financially to your own detriment, enabling your
partner's financial immaturity, or feeling responsible for others' financial
mismanagement. Financial codependency can also look like generosity
that is designed to control—trying to fix problems for others, especially
in ways that are designed to reflect well upon you. Or using money to
curate an image of perfection (having the right car, address, clothes, and
so on) due to an excessive reliance on other people for validation and a
sense of identity. You may also see this arise in never wanting to say no
to an activity even if you can't afford it—spending money on things you
don't care about, such as meals out, concerts, or travel, in order to make
other people happy or gain their approval.

We begin healing codependency when we take full responsibility for
ourselves, our finances, and our decisions and require others to do the
same. This can be extremely painful and difficult if you are a source of
financial support and stability within a family unit, so please make space
for your own guilt, anger, resentment, and confusion to arise in the process of setting boundaries. Get support in meeting these feelings as they
arise and know they are completely normal. This is not about cutting off
people you care about or who depend on you; it is about inviting healthful material interdependency from a grounded, self-loving place.

Low Self-Esteem

Even when you believe you can change, and you recognize your healing
capacity, you may still struggle with low self-esteem. I do and I work on
it on an ongoing basis. I reached a point in my process a few years back,
recovering from the worst breakup of my life, where I knew what I was
seeing in myself was low self-esteem and insecurity, but it confused me
because I was also so confident and liked myself a lot. I was trying to
reconcile this complexity in therapy, as I was grappling with wanting
to keep showing up to process with my ex and be kind and loving even
though I didn't feel like they were treating me in a way that warranted

it. My therapist told me, "You are also in a relationship with yourself."
I was like, *yeah, yeah I get it.* When you're in a breakup, everyone wants
to be like, "Love yourself! Masturbate! Be your own romantic partner!"
and I'm not saying it's not smart, but I am saying that it's annoying.

What unfolded in the conversation next was truly life-changing for
me. She told me that what she meant is that I am building a relationship
to myself by observing my own behavior. Me showing up to process isn't
a stamp of approval of my ex's behavior; I show up because I want to be
a person who treats relationships with the respect and honor I feel they
deserve, who is honoring how significant the relationship was to me. We
build our self-esteem in the same way we build our esteem of anyone
else—by observing how we act and what that says about our values and
our character: Do we do what we say we're going to do? Do our actions
align with our priorities? Are we acting carefully with the things that
matter to us?

So what I'm saying to you is, do the things you say you're going to do.
Make an effort toward your dreams. Treat yourself carefully. Get your
ass on the path to understanding what real resourced self-love looks
and feels like. You are watching how you move, and you are deciding
whether you trust yourself or not. Stop behaving in reaction to other
people, and start behaving based on what will make you feel proud of
yourself. This is how you build up your self-esteem.

Unhelpful Habits

Life is a hustle, and in however many years you've been in charge of
your finances, you're sure to have picked up a bad habit or two. This is
a shame-free zone, so we can lovingly call those habits "unhelpful" and
thank them for the role they have served in our life before we kick them
to the curb. Those neural pathways are not the boss of you! We all want
to feel like we're acting from a place of agency and in our best interest,
and it can be frustrating and even scary when we see the ways we don't.

Lucky for us, there are about a million articles out there on how to hack our brains and break a habit that we no longer desire to have. Learn about the cycle of a habit—cue, routine, reward—and how to disrupt it in order to introduce more choice into your behavior.

MONEY WITCH HOMEWORK

Make a To-Do List

Choose one financial challenge that you are currently facing. This might be paying down credit card debt, getting your student loans out of default, curbing overspending, or needing a higher-earning job.

Out of the list in this chapter, identify three blocks that you feel are impacting this particular challenge the most.

Commit to a path of action on this item. Find tools in the next chapter that will help you make a plan. Break down your plan into tiny, actionable steps, and keep following through.

Money Misogyny

So many of the items our culture categorizes as frivolous spending, that people feel shame about spending money on, are femme items. We feel shame about cruising for clothes and home decor, nail polish and makeup, and skin care and hair care. We have to listen to monotonous discourse about lattes and avocado toast. Those fatty acids make my skin look good! I've never seen an article in mainstream finance say, "It's all those video games and beers that really add up." Clients often have stories about being shamed by their parents for wanting money for femme things. People's partners shame their femme spending. Enough! It's gross.

If you weren't allowed to express or form this part of your identity early in life, shopping can become an avenue for empowerment in adulthood. Which is all good, until you're accumulating debt or using money that your higher self would like to put toward another cause, such as savings. Definitely create intentional space in your budget for femme creativity if it's a priority to you; just make sure it fits within your spending guidelines. Sometimes it's this frustrated, injured, or understimulated part of ourselves that can fall into overspending. When you acknowledge and recognize your inner femme creative and give her intentional space to do her thing, she can stop wreaking havoc on your spending. This can mean using an app like Pinterest to curate outfits and explore aesthetics, cutting and collaging from fashion magazines, getting a Barbie and making her clothes, sketching nail art designs in your journal—whatever you want!

JOURNAL PROMPT
Building Blocks
Which blocks resonate with you? Where do you see yourself and your behavior described in this chapter?

Overinvestment in the Spiritual Idea of Manifestation

Spiritual babes make things happen. We don't always know why or how it went down, but somehow the mystical Universe covers our ass just when we need money to pay a bill. Those of us who have experienced this type of magic can be hesitant to really get involved in the gritty details of financial management, worried we are going to turn it into a

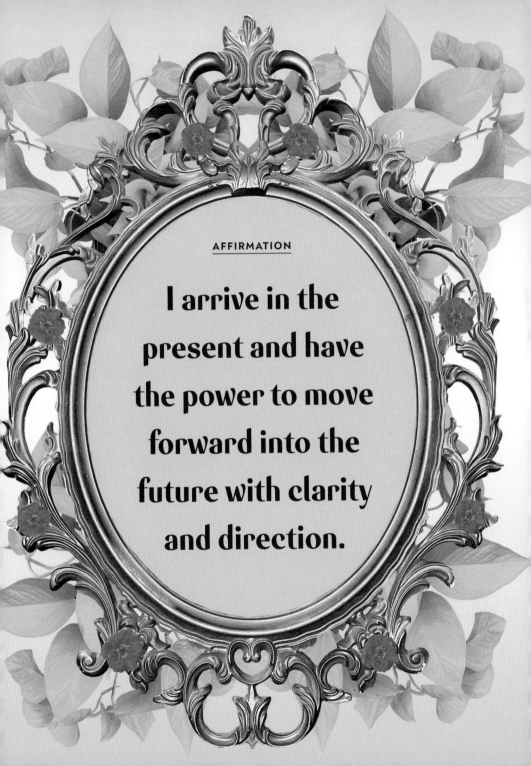

AFFIRMATION

I arrive in the present and have the power to move forward into the future with clarity and direction.

nonspiritual corner of our life, that Spirit will perceive us as greedy or not trusting, or that we'll mess up the flow.

Remember back to the first chapter of this book when we talked about the Three Angles of Healing. Work your magic, but work your practical hustle too. The two are absolutely not mutually exclusive. Let me say this loud and clear. The Universe wants you to participate in making things happen for yourself. G-d is not mad at you for getting involved, and actually walking the walk is how you communicate to the Universe that you're ready to receive the blessing you're asking for.

Cord Cutting

Sitting peacefully and comfortably, call to mind one of the blocks that you identified yourself struggling with.

Think of the block and how it has manifested in your life. Notice how this behavior or attitude was formed as a coping mechanism and thank it for serving you, helping you keep safe and survive. Declare out loud that you are ending your relationship with this block, that your connection to it is forever severed and that you release it completely.

You may take your release work further using one of the three following methods:

- Write the block on a piece of paper, put it in a fireproof bowl, such as a stainless steel kitchen bowl, and light the paper on fire. This action invokes the elements of fire and air to release your relationship with the block.
- Run your hand all over your body, imagining your hand as a sacred sword cutting you free from your attachment to this energy.
- While thinking of the block, scan your body to notice where you feel a connection or cording to this behavior or attitude. Use a ritual blade, a knife, scissors, or a sharp stone to cut through the energy cord between you and this survival mechanism.

Call your energy back to you, becoming more potent and healed, ready to move forward differently.

STEP

6

The Tools, Helping You
Help Yourself

---

*Build the toolbox you
need to address and heal
your financial blocks.*

MONEY MAGIC ALLIES

Astrological Role Model

Capricorn: Capricorn, characterized as a sea-goat, knows that there's nowhere to go but up and no way to get there but climb. Conquering obstacles is not a necessary evil; it's the whole game of life. And Capricorn is going to win. Cap has climbed as far up the cliffs as it has plunged into the depths of the watery sea. The emotional deep diving is an essential step of the process, but not a place to stay long term. Capricorn wants you to take all those pearls you found, get them set into some fly-ass jewelry, and go out on the town to win over hearts, wallets, and accolades.

Crystal Friends

Lepidolite: Called the stone of peace, this lilac-gray stone contains mood-stabilizing lithium to relieve the paralytic effects of stress, anxiety, and depression. If you experience difficulty in making money due to emotional pain, lepidolite can help. This mineral calms nervous brain patterns, such as negative self-talk or future-tripping, allowing you to be present with only the current moment. This pause in the whirlwind of anxiety allows reorganization of old behavioral and thinking patterns, gently inducing change.

Tigereye: The stripes in this golden-brown stone bring alignment to help you get your life in order! Bringing mental clarity and insight into complicated situations, tigereye helps you sort through everything on your mind and get it all put away neatly in the metaphoric filing cabinet. It helps you seek and implement effective solutions, informed but not clouded by your emotions. As it also promotes wealth, money, and luck, this is the perfect stone to utilize in organizing your finances.

Tiny Tarot Reading

Temperance and The Magician: You've always been powerful, but now your journey has deepened and your spiritual self has become stronger. You are an artist in every area of your life, so create the environment you want to exist within. Take what you've learned and alchemize change in your material circumstances. Apply all your gained self-awareness to balance the spiritual and the economic with grace. Don't forget that you have Spirit on your side and you are magical beyond measure when you put your mind to it.

Cup of Tea

A daily tonic of nettles, red clover, alfalfa, and spearmint will build and resource you.

Every job is easier when you have the right tools. In this step, we will obtain the tools to dismantle your blocks, giving you the resources to do the work. This work of dismantling and rebuilding your inner relationship to money is what frees your energy up to take action.

It can be easy to get caught up in the mental side of healing—contextualizing, learning, and understanding. Don't lose sight of the fact that our goal is to take these lessons to implementation. Making even one actionable change in your life after reading this book will be worth more than trying to dissect or understand every emotional and spiritual lesson contained within it. Don't feel pressure to remember or internalize this whole book. Instead, commit to one to three actionable things that you will shift. Use the tools in this chapter as a jumping-off point to get the resources you need, gathering and acquiring emotional skills like a boss until you've got an abundantly full money magic toolbox.

INTRODUCING . . . THE TOOLS!

Cultivate Financial Intimacy*

You build intimacy with your finances the same way you build intimacy in any relationship: Show up regularly, be present, pay attention, and care about the needs of the relationship. Then, check back in often enough that you can discern when needs arise and respond to the best of your ability and capacity. When you have an intimate relationship with your money, you can move with it responsively, quickly, and agilely. You can make the best micro-decisions and form your path as you move, rather than having to go back and correct huge pieces of your course

---

* I first heard the term *financial intimacy* from the book *Financial Intimacy: How to Create a Healthy Relationship with Your Money and Your Mate*, by Jacquette M. Timmons, a Black female investment expert and financial coach. You should definitely buy this book to learn how to talk and navigate with your intimate partner around money. #citeblackwomen

that you traveled with too little information. Financial intimacy is the antidote for avoidance.

We all know there's a huge difference in friends we talk to every day and friends we catch up with only every six months or year. The biggest difference is that friends we are in regular contact with know much more about the intricacies of our needs, and we know much more about theirs too. Get in BFF status with your money so you can help each other out through this thing called life.

Embrace Financial Literacy

Literacy enlivens and transforms us; it creates relevance and engagement. It makes the context of money, the ecosystem of money, the language of money come alive for us. And we learn language just like a baby does, by engaging and taking small daily steps until we gain mastery. Apply this theory of small, constant exposure to the language of your finances.

Learn about what you are engaged in financially: how much is in your accounts, how much your income and expenses are, how much is in your wallet, how much you owe and to whom, how much savings you have and where. Literacy is how you make something legible to yourself. If your finances feel illegible to you, you will continue to feel distant from them. Start relating to money as something you care about understanding.

Build Financial Self-Esteem

As we talked about in the blocks section (page 128), you have to operate in a way you respect so that you can build your positive self-image. Taking action is good for your self-esteem. When you notice yourself doing things like paying your bills on time, checking your account balance before you make a purchase, maxing out your 401(k) matching contribution from your employer, and keeping up on your small-business bookkeeping, you make yourself proud. You impress yourself. And you form an image of yourself as the type of person who takes care of their finances. This may be a type of person you could never have imagined yourself being, but you are totally well on your way.

Do what you need to do and do it impeccably. This alignment will bring you the truest experience of empowerment.

Reparent for Real

A lot of us have met our injured inner children at therapy. They throw tantrums when we're trying to date, want chicken nuggets when we're trying to eat raw vegan, and spend all our retirement money in the $1 bin at Target. They are sweet and precious, and it's not their fault they didn't get their needs met.

It's a bummer for absolute sure, but at this point, we are adults and the time to get our childhood needs met has past. We are left with the wreckage of neglect, abuse, or mismanagement. We are, deep sigh, responsible for ourselves. The parts of us that didn't get taken care of in a way that was fulfilling are the problem children in the classroom of our psyche, but now we are the teacher. It takes some real acknowledgment and grieving to process losing the opportunity for a resourced childhood. Seeing and validating those sweet, sad babes is the first part of the process. Then we have to get down to the work of reparenting them.

So what does reparenting your inner child look like in a financial context? It's liberating our own idea of love, and expanding our techniques of self-love and self-care beyond the bounds of the ways we were raised. Check in with any ways you may be perpetuating patterns of neglect or spoiling in your self-care. Let's widen our definition of self-care to include handling the difficult things. Let's push ourselves to a form of self-care that engages self-love, not just self-soothing. Self-care means giving ourselves the tools we need to live our lives with reduced stress and drama, not just managing the symptoms of that stress and drama.

Our go-to self-care strategies are often designed to make us feel good in the moment, or to recover from stressful situations, but there are so many other aspects to love besides soothing and comfort—and a huge part of parenting is about ensuring safety, having a plan, and meeting material needs.

AFFIRMATION

I care about my money, so I put in work to understand it better.

Financial reparenting looks like this:

PLANNING FOR THE FUTURE: Believing in yourself, your goals, and your potential. Think about what you'll need five, ten, thirty years down the line. What are your dreams and what resources do you need to make them happen?

SAVING FOR EMERGENCIES: Making sure the precious person you're in charge of will never be left without their basic needs met.

PAYING ATTENTION TO YOUR BASIC PROVISIONS: Financially prioritizing stocking healthy, accessible, appealing food options. If your socks and underwear have holes in them, throw them out and get new ones. Make sure you put money and time aside for dental and vision care. Get your tires checked.

ASSESSING YOUR BASELINE NEEDS: Having the maturity to explore what deeper need is asking to be met when your inner child is screaming for sushi or new toys—do they actually need connection, a snuggle, to experience boundaries and safety, to have someone listen to and witness their experience?

My definition of spoiling in a caretaking context is giving a kid what they want but not what they need. The key to killing it at reparenting is to look at what your inner child really needs. When we spend our money on things that we want at the cost of what we need in the name of self-care, we are engaging in wounded caretaking. We may be replicating caretakers or parents in our life who didn't have the emotional capacity to give us what we really needed and supplemented that by giving us material treats and comforts. We may be modeling our idea of what it looks like to love ourselves on the neglectful care we received. No shame to our wounded caregivers here either, but let's do better, as we know better. Just like those who raised us, we are stressed, under-resourced, and dealing with some wild shit. When your inner child starts yelling about feeling neglected, it's easier to buy her some nail polish or some French fries than to look at what would really nourish her emotional and physical safety, but I promise the payout is massive. Be a good caretaker to yourself, and prioritize the things that will help you feel safe and resourced in this world. When we bring our injured inner child up to speed, we get to walk as a fully integrated person and be free from our past.

Stop Punishing Yourself

Our mind on money can be a downward spiral of regrets and mistakes looped over and over. It may activate fear of our future missteps. Some anxiety is fueled by guilt. Some is a punishment for past mistakes, subconsciously believing you deserve a bit of self-flagellation. We think we deserve to feel bad or be punished because of things we've done or ways we "are." This type of thinking and acting is antithetical to the world we want to usher in. Undoing systems of supremacy ultimately means undoing systems of value. When we strive to be "good," we are seeking a cookie, maybe from ourselves. We are looking for something that says we deserve to be alive and to exist; we are looking to prove it. Liberate your healing process from moralism.

Consult Your Astrological Chart

Astrology is a system of archetypes that assists us in building self-awareness. In my view of astrology, your astrological chart (also sometimes called your birth chart or natal chart) is your evolutionary curriculum. It's as close as you're going to get to an instruction manual for your life, and who doesn't want one of those? Your astrological chart is essentially a blueprint of your interiority. If you work with your natal chart already, don't forget that it can tell you about the ways you may interact with and be motivated in your relationship with resources. When using your astrological chart to perceive your financial behavior, explore the areas of the chart I call the Earth Journey: the second, sixth, and tenth houses. Which planets are present there, and which signs are they in?

AFFIRMATION

I am building my financial self-esteem by aligning my behaviors with my priorities.

JOURNAL PROMPT
Find Your Midheaven

When looking at your astrological chart to get information about your financial life, an especially important point is the sign on the cusp of the tenth house, which is called your midheaven, and sometimes the "M.C."

Use an online site, such as astro.com, to find your midheaven. The sign your midheaven is in tells you where to orient in order to bring success into your life. Embrace and embody the positive attributes of that sign's archetype in order to see improved success in every area of your life. When you have to make a choice around a course of action, ask yourself, *What would a _____ do?*

In your journal, spend some time exploring your personal definition of success. Where do you feel the most successful in your life? In what part of your finances are you currently experiencing success? What would being financially successful look like to you?

Make Responsibility Sexy

Responsibility can be such a boring and heavy word, but it's the key to all this grown-up stuff, and grown and sexy is a thing, so let's transform our association. When you decline to take responsibility for your life and your commitments out of fear or desire for comfort or ease, you lose out on agency and power. Agency means you're acting on your own behalf instead of asking another to be responsible for acting for you. Basically, getting to do what we want is the good part of adulthood; it's the paycheck for doing the job of taking full responsibility for ourselves.

Responsibility is relational; it shows that you take your relationship to yourself seriously. And also that you take your relationship to others around you seriously by not pushing them to take responsibility for you when you are ultimately capable of taking responsibility for yourself. This is not to downplay interdependency, the sharing of responsibility, or asking others to support us in important ways we may not be able to implement on our own. This is not about taking responsibility or blame for things that are outside of your control, but it is about acknowledging what you do have control over and absolutely rocking it.

Responsibility is different than duty, and being accountable is not an obligation to live out a familial fantasy. Get clear about your commitments, and center your concept of responsibility on honoring your own desires and values. Show honor to yourself and the people who care about you through self-loving behavior. It's superhot.

Claim Abundance

Abundance is the antidote to shame and scarcity. Abundance says there is enough and you are deserving. Good things can, do, and will happen to you. Claim it, out loud, this very minute.

Move your focus away from the lack and the struggle. I know that it is not easy and that there are lots of little things that happen every day that remind you of what you don't have, your philosophy on why you don't have it, and the fight it has taken to get you to where you are now. Again, this work acknowledges the material impact of oppression. You don't have to ignore the circumstances that impact your financial reality, or gaslight yourself into thinking limitations are your fault because you haven't mindset-ed your way out of them.

I also know that allowing yourself space for expansive thinking is key to liberation work. There is more possible than we can even imagine, and we deserve to live in a place that centers that vision and activates our work toward it. Abundance is financial, but it also embraces an abundance of connection, an abundance of equity, an abundance of joy, and an abundance of actualization. Focus here, on these possibilities. Embrace them as your own.

Leverage the Glaze-Over Moment

When you are looking at your bank statement, or trying to read the profit-and-loss statement for your small business, or filling out an application, notice the very instant that you start to glaze over. This means you have stopped absorbing or relating to what your eyes are seeing. The "glaze-over moment" is an indicator that either you are overwhelmed or you have stopped understanding (or both). Confusion can also be a coping mechanism from the past, something your brain has utilized to protect you from trauma.

When you find yourself in the glaze-over moment, stop and pause. It will be uncomfortable, but tolerating purposeful discomfort is essential for growth.

Stay present and track your reactions. The amazing thing about not understanding something is that it offers an opportunity to learn something new. You deserve to understand. Pause in order to identify what it is that you don't understand. It may be as broad as "I don't understand what I'm looking at" or as specific as "I don't know what that transaction was for." Turn your statement into a question, and get your question answered.

If your glaze-over moment does not seem to be springing from lack of understanding, but from a general overwhelm, remember the work of this whole book. What is happening is that a practical interaction with money is activating and excavating hard feelings. Try to listen to your feelings, listen to your internal experience, and use the identification tools we have strengthened in this financial healing journey. Overwhelm feels so big, but really it's just you feeling some feelings. And feelings are more than OK. When you welcome them in rather than pushing them out, you gain knowledge, wisdom, and the ability to metabolize the emotions and move forward.

Heal Your Lineage

If you are tired of the baggage, tired of carrying your family's signature grief around money, get in touch with and engage ancestral healing technologies from your traditions. This involves praying to the deep elder spirits to work down your line generationally toward you. Ask your most ancient ancestors what you can do to assist and fuel their work. As the living, we are in a unique position to support the lineage-healing process.

Do your grieving work. The purpose of grief is to dissolve and dissipate old energies. You are washing away financial suffering and releasing it from your family line. This is for you, for your grandparents, and for your children. What are you done with? What do you no longer want? Decide to let it go. Release it now.

On one side is your past, the ancestors, and on the other side is your future and your descendants. If you struggle to do financial healing for yourself, do it for the lineage called the future. Develop a relationship with your future self, your elder self. Develop a relationship to your future community, your elder community. They need you to create a foundation of stability that will support them. Retirement and savings is radical elder care. Think about what financial baggage has been passed down to you that you would like to liberate your descendants, whether familial or communal, from carrying. Decide what stops with you, in this generation.

Take Yourself on a Money Date

Make time for yourself and time for your money. Pick a time each week that you will have a money date with yourself and schedule it in. Weekly is better than monthly because you will inevitably miss every once in a while and going two months without money check-ins will interrupt your flow. It's easy to go from there to "this just isn't happening anymore." Checking in with your money this regularly will allow you to make micro-choices and respond to your finances with agility and intimacy, which can help you see when you need to change paths. Weekly meetings can also be shorter, which might make them more feasible for your schedule, or you could let yourself skip (only) one per month. Be real with yourself about how slippery of a person you are and make sure you don't permit your way in to a self-sabotage situation. Get your dates on the calendar and consider them nonnegotiable.

Create a lot of pleasure points in your money time—light a special candle, put a nice essential oil in the diffuser, have a fancy snack or a glass of wine. Get pretty file folders and pens. It can lube up the process a little bit to build an association between something you love and a task you need to handle. If you have to bribe yourself with candy to get your ass in a seat and look at your debt, adult to adult, I think that's fine. If your neural pathways begin to associate your money meeting with your favorite ice cream or watching your favorite TV show afterward, that starts to build some motivation. Eventually, getting stuff done and checked off your list and the pride and excitement of having better habits will build momentum.

What are you going to do daily, weekly, monthly, quarterly? Create a rhythm and rock with it.

Money is sexually attracted to you. Money loves you. Money cannot wait to get next to you. Money thinks about you all day, fantasizing about the moment when it gets to rendezvous with you. Embrace this vibration and make it yours. Stand in a deep attractiveness and recep-tivity to money. Explore any ways that you notice resistance to money, to resources, and to wealth within your body and your spirit. Create an inviting internal atmosphere for money to enter. Embrace the intimacy and sensuality of your money date.

Utilize Containers, Compartmentalization, and Boundaries

One of the great things about setting aside specific time and space to deal with your finances head-on is that it means you get to allow yourself real space from them the rest of the time. Like we said when we talked about avoidance, all putting tasks off really does is mean it's always on your to-do list. Having a container means that the process can start to live within a boundary rather than spilling all over everything in your life. Containers also mean there is somewhere to put your money process. Everyone who keeps a house clean knows that if an item doesn't have a place that it lives, it will just float around in a perpetual state of making a mess. Same with your tasks and processes. For example, the money meeting is a container. When financial tasks arise during the week (I should call my student loan company, or I need to pay xyz bills), they go on the money meeting list. You know when and where you'll handle them so they won't nag at you every day until then. As you utilize containers longer, the system becomes stronger and you will be able to trust it more, which can drastically reduce anxiety. When financial stressors arise, you can see and acknowledge their presence but you don't have to hold them intimately until meeting time.

Be Selfish

If you grew up in a marginalized body, particularly with regard to race, class, immigration status, and/or gender, spend some time regularly not giving a single fuck about what you can do for others. Create a disciplined practice of identifying, planning for, and focusing on your personal goals, led by your personal desires. What are the things that need to happen to get you to your dreams? This is not about actualizing other people's agenda for you, only about following your own divinely verified path.

Invest money in the tools and education you need to advance your projects. Give your time to yourself through meditation, visioning, self-care rituals, and rest. Allot creativity to your own passion projects and hobbies rather than expending it all at work. Make sure your own needs get on the agenda. Hydrate, moisturize, stretch, and schedule a dental appointment. Call your energy back from the relationships, causes, conflicts, and frustrations it may be scattered to. Build sanctuary space for yourself, even if it's a tiny altar tucked away somewhere. Visit it regularly and get centered and grounded before you face the world.

Get Some Money Manners

A lot of us who grew up with race, gender, and/or class privilege have terrible boundaries. We also have low expectations for our own behavior, and pretty bad manners. If you are working on healing entitlement and privilege, put some work into checking the ways you act when you are seeking access to someone's time, resources, ideas, and energy. Right relationship, a core principle of the Quaker religion, is essential to all interactions, and the world of money is full of transactions and interactions. Right relationship includes not just asking before you take something, but thinking before even asking. Can you do it for yourself? Can you search that question on the internet? If you need help, consider both your position of privilege and your relationship to the person you're asking. No one can pay their rent with good will, "exposure," or warm fuzzies. Being offered a chance to help you do something is different than being offered a valuable and lucrative opportunity. Show recognition, gratitude, and reciprocity. Say it with access, opportunity, and cash.

Try Somatic Healing

Somatic healing refers to several lineages of therapy, movement, and touch designed to activate healing through the connection of mind and body. If you tend to be cognitive, holding everything up in your mind while struggling to connect with your body, these modalities can provide profound healing. Somatic practices can also find stored trauma and outdated nervous system responses that are difficult to access with verbal modalities, such as talk therapy or tarot readings.

Your body is an amazing sensitive thermometer. Any time you do anything with money, or money related, check in with what your body is doing. Practice stopping, noticing, and resetting.

Cultivate Discipline

As an Aries with ADD, I have basically no place speaking on this except to say I struggle with it every day! Discipline has been one of the greatest lessons in my life, and is the thing that makes my dreams and visions come true. I believe it can do the same for you. I live by the adage

"Discipline is remembering what you want." Depending on your history, discipline can be subconsciously tied in your mind to punishment. It can invoke sensations of deprivation and scarcity, but it's actually just about staying focused on the things that are important to you. The structure that you create is the bones of your life—what prop up and allow the sexier, funner parts to function well.

I love a shiny thing, but I love my end game and goals more, so cultivating discipline is key. Your purpose, path, and vision are precious, so make them the center focal point of your life. Bringing a daily practice of spiritual or artistic discipline into your life, such as meditation, movement, writing, or making art, builds these muscles and allows you to approach other issues, such as your finances, with enhanced fortitude and focus.

Discipline is the practice of focus, and strategy is the framework of focus. Strategy is all about what we say yes and no to. It means paying attention to what actions will take you closer or further away from your goal and choosing the steps in your intended direction. Other things may be appealing, but they do not contribute to the goal. Stick to the strategic plan, but don't get trapped in rigidity—you are always free to revise your intentions, goals, and plans, and you should definitely be auditing those categories regularly to make sure they are current and relevant.

Create a strategy for each financial goal you are aiming to actualize. Use the principle of "first things first": Prioritize the one action that will have the most impact, or the thing that will put other steps in motion. Reverse-engineer your goals and lay them out on a time line. For example, if you want to save $1,000 for a birthday trip in six months, break it down and make specific time-bound commitments to actualizing your plan. In this particular situation, setting aside $45 a week, or $90 per pay period, would take you to your goal. Discipline looks like setting this money aside first each time you get paid, before you start ordering takeout or buying houseplants.

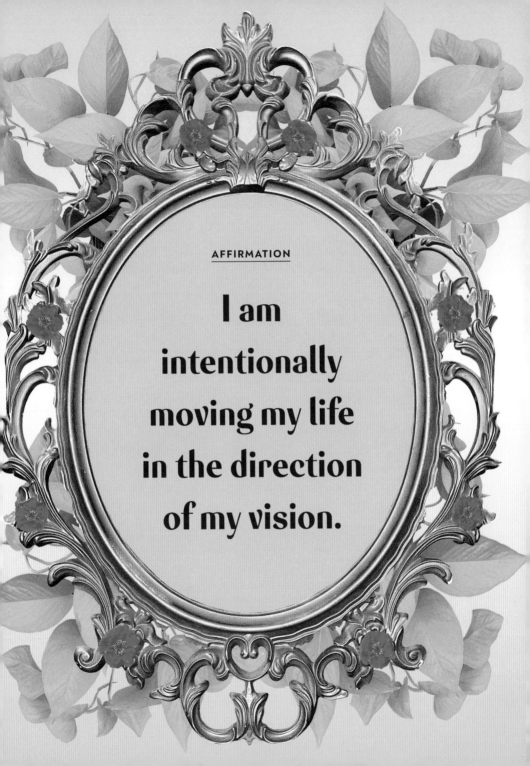

AFFIRMATION

I am intentionally moving my life in the direction of my vision.

The idea of a time line becomes even more important when the goal is complex. If you figure out when your earlier steps need to get executed and stick with it, you'll be at ease and lower-stress later on. Remember how we're not cultivating crisis for ourselves? Say your goal is to launch an herbal product in six months. Reverse-engineer your plan from there. When do you need the labels and bottles to arrive so that you can get your product photography for the web store? How much shipping time does the printer take, and therefore when do you need to order the labels? What does that mean about when the graphic design process has to be over, so when does it have to start? How long will it take you to write the copy for the designer to use in the label design? To solidify that copy, you have to have the product formula locked down. Putting your goals on a time line and following through with the plan means you're intentionally moving your life in the direction of your vision.

Seek Culturally Affirming Professionals and Resources

Work with financial professionals who will meet you where you are if at all possible. If your banker, lawyer, or investment broker doesn't know how to speak in a respectful tone of voice, or how to break things down in a way that works for you, then fire their ass. If you don't feel like the money podcast you started listening to gets your experience, and it makes you feel ashamed or alienated, stop listening. Just don't shut down and give up at that point. The important part is to keep pushing, seeking, and advocating for resources that are resonant and relevant. There are an increasing number of financial educators and resources whose focus is to lift up marginalized people's financial access, so ask around to find someone who is the right fit for you.

Get Excited about Reality!

Reframe your existence. This is that one amazing human life that you have been dealt. This is your time to burn bright like the stardust that you are. Even though life on Earth in your particular form can feel like a drag, you have been born perfectly into this lifetime. No one else could play your part. You've been written in to the human story, cast in the role, and pushed out on stage whether you feel ready or not, so I suggest you put on some makeup, get a great costume, and give the performance of, well, a lifetime.

Build a Money Altar

Altars are a cross-cultural, diasporic technology for accessing the spirituality of your ancestors. Your ancestors had special places they could go to talk to Spirit. This may have been a temple, a sacred grove, or a rock formation. As many people of the Earth no longer live in, or have access to, the place where their ancestors talked to Spirit (due to migration, colonialism, displacement, or choice), we have had to find new ways and new places to have these conversations. The altars in our homes are our places to converse with Spirit and to make offerings to our ancestors, Spirit, angels, and guides. Stand at your altar and pray, and tend to it daily. You will find a spark of your ancestors inside you.

Altar work can be extremely effective because it holds space for spiritual reflection, cultivates regular practice (a.k.a. discipline), and creates reminders of our intentions. This can include an intention to live a more spiritual lifestyle or to deepen your relationship to the Divine. An altar can fill the human need to see your internal experience reflected back to you. Actively allowing ourselves to be mirrored soothes and nurtures our baby selves, who use this experience to develop both self-esteem and empathy. Nurturing our baby selves and child selves allows us to act from a place of maturity in the rest of our lives. Through this self-soothing, we get to stay rooted and grounded in a secure place and access our capacity to connect to others. Allow your altar to help you feel seen, represented, and reflected.

Having a specific money altar reflects that you are serious and focused about activating and sustaining change in this area of your life. What you pay attention to grows, so show your money the respect you'd like it to show you.

People always want to know "the right way" to set up an altar, but ultimately there is no wrong way to set one up. If you follow a particular lineage, listen to the guidelines of that tradition. The greatest source of information will be the conversation between your intuition and the altar itself. Set up the space and then listen to the information that comes to you about what you should add, change, move, or remove. This information may come as an idea that crosses your mind, something you've read or heard from multiple sources, a dream, or a strong feeling that something is just "right" or "off."

To begin setting up your money altar, choose a location, either for practical reasons (a.k.a. there's room here) or vibrational reasons (in your work space, in an area designated as a wealth zone by your spiritual/ancestral traditions).

Lay down a cloth that feels rich to you—gold, any metallic, red, purple, velvet, fabric printed with cash or coins, and so on. Then choose what items to place on your altar. When you have a problem you need to talk out, you may seek a specific person in your life based on the issue. In the same way, you will get the most help if you choose the crystal, plant, or other element with the right "personality" to help you with your specific concern or journey. Just like the human world, the natural world contains a full spectrum of vibrations. It can help to identify which friends in the natural and archetypal worlds (elements, plants, crystals, planets, birds, animals, tarot cards, astrological glyphs, deities) have a vibration that aligns with what you are seeking in your financial life and then ask those friends to help you in your work by placing icons of them on your altar. Reintroduce yourself to the money magic allies from the beginning of each chapter. Write any affirmations that especially resonated with you on a card, and place them on your altar.

Remember that your money altar is a living, changing entity, not a diorama. Engage with it, be in conversation with it, and switch it up as your goals, challenges, and desires change.

STEP

7

Try. Definitely Fail.

Try Again.

Cocreate with the Universe by aligning your actions with your intentions.

MONEY MAGIC ALLIES

Astrological Role Model

Aries: As the first sign of the zodiac cycle, Aries is the initial spark that starts the engine. Aries is the primal creative action. All life stems from Aries springing forth. Aries knows that newness and rebirth are not only possible but also an inevitable part of life. This knowledge imbues Aries with courage and the bravery to try again. Aries is the warrior, who truly excels when it's time to face a challenge and make a move. Channel your inner warrior to embody honorable assertiveness and aggression against that which keeps you stuck. You have the power to create positive change.

Crystal Friends

Gold: Gold represents the sacred origins of all money, all energy, and all life. It represents the intention of exchange, mutuality, and relationship that is at the core of money. Gold channels the energy of the sun, which is the source of all life on Earth. When you use money, you make a decision to engage in a sacred exchange, sharing your life force with another. Call on gold when you need to remember that your money work is your spiritual work.

Carnelian: This red-brown stone taps into your base and supports the root of your work. It builds a stable and forceful foundation for your action, making it seem less intimidating and more manageable. Carnelian motivates steady action, building intentionally toward success. Call on it to dissolve apathy, move forward with confidence, and activate grounded success in every area of your life.

Tiny Tarot Reading

Strength and The Fool: This power pair says love is the source of your strength and the source of all action. Root every action in love. Make your money moves based on love for yourself. Your efforts also show love for the world, as the human community needs you to be healing and empowered. Find yourself worthy of a fresh start, release your inhibitions, and act courageously. There is always space to try again. Every time you start a journey, you bring new wisdom and experience to your toolbox. Notice the insight you have gathered from everything you've been through. Appreciate the opportunity to try again. You are so much more capable now.

A Cup of Tea

Ginger and nettles will help you move away from stagnation and get the support and nourishment you need to keep going.

The work you do on this journey has the power to change your life if you let it. Let the healing that you have done sink in to every cell of your body and let it move through you into your sphere of action. But treat yourself gently. This process of financial growth is not a compulsory chore; this is not another should. This work is for you, born out of love for yourself, born out of the belief that you can have more, that security and abundance and integrity are for you. Take action out of this same self-love. Be caring and build something of value for yourself. You deserve it.

A great plan is not one that ticks off the boxes on some model citizen checklist. A great plan is one that is actually going to get done, a plan that you are not going to (want to) avoid. Getting out of our heads and into our bodies can be challenging. Developing an analysis and shifting your mindset is one part of transformation. We spent this journey together wrestling with the emotions that surround our financial lives. The next part of transformation is to harness the understanding we have gained to right our path of action.

In step 7, we will move into the action realm, taking everything we learned, all our powerful revelation built on deep awareness of our unique self and situation, and alchemizing it into movement. Changing just one thing about the way you do money can change the whole trajectory of your journey with material resources. Giving yourself permission to get better and get different will liberate you from so much pain and struggle. Our goal in this chapter is to get your actions in alignment with your intentions and your desires, and give Spirit a place to work miracles in your life.

Show up and blow up. You have totally got this.

THE BLESSING UNFOLDS
IN YOUR ACTIONS

My dears, when I say the blessing unfolds in your actions, I mean you must get your tush in alignment with what you are asking for. The Universe pays attention to what you say with your words but even more so to what you say with your actions and effort. If you are telling the Universe you are ready to buy a house, and you are writing that intention in a manifestation journal, you are doing a spell. Then you must also do the spell of opening a savings account to build up your down payment. You must do the spell of putting money away for your new home, even if that's $20 a week. What matters is that it is substantial to you individually.

Your efforts are a spell; your efforts are a ritual. Pray with your efforts. Manifest with your efforts. We can't control if it rains, but if we don't plant seeds, there will definitely be no crops. Plant seeds of financial growth in the dark fertile soil of your life, tend to them, and watch your manifestations grow strong and unstoppable.

TRY AND FAIL

The thing about taking action is that we are going to mess up. We are going to falter. We are going to hit places of stagnation, and we are most definitely going to make mistakes. Taking action is one thing, but dusting yourself off after a bump and taking action again is the ticket to really finding success. You deserve the opportunity to try, but you truly deserve the opportunity to fail and try again.

I internalized this lesson the hard way, and almost shut down my business in the process.

The year 2014 was the first full year of Money Witch, and I spent it working slowly, doing bookkeeping and business strategy for a couple of friends and some word-of-mouth clients. I decided at the end of the year that 2015 was going to be the year things would really take off for me:

I was going to open up to a larger batch of tax clients and build a real practice for myself.

I was excited and also scared as hell, but I was ready to go. Then in January 2015 a client for whom I had prepared taxes contacted me to let me know she was being audited by the IRS. In hindsight, this wasn't a huge deal. It's just a thing that happens sometimes and often is a much less dramatic process than it's made out to be in the popular imagination. An audit means that the IRS has questions about some numbers on your return and wants additional information to back them up. It's like the math teacher asking you to show your work. At the time, though, I was pretty terrified, not to mention defensive and deeply questioning my skills. On top of it all, this client was working in a criminalized industry, which made her whole return more high-stakes.

I apologized (probably inadequately) and prepared to help in any way I could. But my client didn't want my help. She had lost trust in me. There will always be someone or something that reflects your deepest insecurities back to you, and she really nailed it. I saw those dreaded words glaring back from the computer screen: I just think you're representing yourself as more competent than you really are.

I was devastated and completely ashamed and embarrassed. I wanted to shut down my business. Everything in my body was telling me that I wasn't skilled enough to do this work and that I was bound to keep fucking up, violating people's expectations of me. I am so grateful that I chose to give myself a gift at that moment. The gift was that I noticed a tiny ember inside of me that was whispering, *It's OK to make a mistake. What do you need to learn in order not to make this same mistake again?* I poured all my discomfort into understanding the problem that had occurred and researching how to not make it again. I read books about audits and I figured out what I would go back and change if I could. I talked it out with my friends and my mom until I could identify what I needed to take responsibility for and what was being projected onto me by an angry, scared client. I gave myself the experience of redemption that my client had denied me. I came out feeling stronger,

AFFIRMATION

I act in
alignment with
my highest
good.

more knowledgeable, and more ready to navigate both the world of taxes and the world of client management. I also came out accepting that I am human, and I'm not obligated to be flawless, even if that's my clients' hope.

Money Witch was built brick by brick over time. This business is an absolute journey. It still grows organically and slowly, with lots of stops and starts. I've had bursts of growth and periods of rest and plateau. Most of the time when an endeavor becomes more publicly well known, the person behind the scenes has been grinding and building for years to make it happen. My business wasn't a perfectly engineered exercise; it's an ongoing conversation between me, as a person who is growing and becoming, and my clientele. I didn't launch at six figures and, seven years in, I'm still striving to make the kind of income I want for myself—one that will allow me to save tons for retirement, abundantly support people and organizations that are making a liberated world possible, handle emergencies without financial crisis, have stability and agency in my housing and transportation, and give me the expendable income to buy cute outfits so I look great doing it.

I share this story to remind you that stumbling is part of the process. You're going to fuck up. Like not just make a little mistake, like really fuck up. Hurt someone you care about. Behave in a way that appalls you. Get someone audited by the IRS. Feel ashamed and like you want to disappear. Start a business that ends up shutting down, lose investors, go into debt. You're going to make a bad investment, maybe get a little scammed, quit your job or drop out of your degree program and then regret it, miss an opportunity. It's OK.

The world is ready to accept you in all your mistakes and all your efforts. Let her hold you when you miss the mark, knowing that next time you will act with more information and more grace. Grace is the key. Grace is the balance of striving and effort with acceptance and surrender. Grace is resilient. Grace means embracing what you have to work with and integrating new information as it comes. Grace makes it look good. Grace is you being you to the fullest, knowing that there's no other possible way to be. Grace means accepting when things are not for you and walking away from them. Grace means elegantly accepting the blessings that are yours and not dodging them.

JOURNAL PROMPT

No Fear

What fears stop you from taking action? Choose one action you'd like to take to better your financial life, and then list the fears you must face in order to see your actions manifest.

REVELATION
AND REDEMPTION

Not believing that we deserve to make a mistake or be messy is shame rearing its head, because it means not believing we deserve to be human. Whether or not we believe that we deserve a shot at redemption after we make mistakes, we have to accept that the process is unavoidable and we cause ourselves pain by not participating in it. What do we gain by punishing ourselves and denying ourselves a chance to repair our mistakes? Punishment can scratch the itch of shame a little bit. I may feel that I am doing some sort of penance for myself or my ancestors by suffering, but the truth is that my emotional pain does not increase the quality of a single person's life or legacy. It is of no tangible value. What my suffering does is keep me stuck, and when I'm stuck I can't do anything to create amends, apologize, be accountable, or change the course of the situation. The only opportunity that suffering produces is inflicting enough pain to cause a breakthrough. Allow your heart to open up, allow yourself to be broken open. Be vulnerable and care. Care about yourself, your life, your future, your finances. Care about having your most actualized life.

I spent a good portion of my thirties thinking that it was possible to just devour enough information to stay ahead of the curve, and self-enlighten and analyze my way out of making any mistakes that would hurt the people I love. I couldn't imagine that people in my life would make space for me to make mistakes, that they could forgive me, that they could love me through it. How could I possibly deserve it?

The thing is that you don't have to do a single thing to deserve redemption. There is no such thing as deserving it. Deserve means there's a judge, and that there's a hierarchical system that we accept. As we become vessels for the new world that is birthing and returning to herself, we have to reject every system that places humans as more or less deserving of resources, and that includes rejecting the idea that redemption is impossible.

We are born and live life with a pure soul, a spark of light, placed within us by Creator. This pure soul is a place to which we can always return, our inner reset button. To be born, to receive revelation, and to receive redemption—this is the passing of time. We are created, we learn by mistake, we get to try again, sometimes with a little more ease. We create, we reveal, we redeem. We participate in others' redemption by forgiving mistakes. We participate in our own redemption by aligning ourselves with the revelations we receive, by returning to ourselves, by forgiving ourselves. We apologize, we ask for forgiveness, we return to our highest selves. The pure light of the Creator shines through you in every action and is radiated even in your mistakes.

Notice yourself approaching a vantage point or a challenge point where you have stood in the past and observe yourself feeling differently, reacting differently, enacting change that supports your move to get in greater integrity. Time is both cyclical and linear, creating a spiral of existence. Each time you notice that you are at a similar point in the cycle, you will also notice that you have moved forward as well, empowered by revelation, closer to redemption. Although *redemption* has a Judeo-Christian connotation of being saved from sin, I love the *Oxford English Dictionary* definition, which is "the action of regaining or gaining

possession of something in exchange for payment, or clearing a debt."
When we heal, we are clearing a debt, an ancestral debt, an evolutionary
debt of our soul, a debt we have accumulated through years of acting
out of alignment, acting in coping strategies. We end up with deferred
maintenance of the self. When we return to the Divine, when we return
to our highest self, when we grapple with the shadow, when we integrate
all our selves, we clear our self of that debt. We may clear any number
of ancestors' and descendants' debt along with it. Through this payment
of the labor of healing, we regain possession of something, and that
something is nothing less than the totality of ourself. Healing will cause
suffering, but then it will create so much peace and empowerment.

Make a commitment to prioritize your own healing. Your personal
healing is intertwined with the healing of the collective. We all need to
be healing in order to be able to participate and show up. Sometimes
the absolute best thing you can do for the collective is to meditate and
ground yourself before going out to that community meeting, party, or
event. The same is true in this financial healing process—the best thing
you can do for collective economic liberation is to clean up your own
financial house. This doesn't mean just focus on getting more for you;
this means putting in the work to untangle your money—both your
mindset and your material landscape—so that you are living abundantly,
generously, and in alignment with your values. Yes, make sure you are
striking a balance and staying accountable to the collective and to the
needs of people more marginalized than you are. Your healing is revolutionary if you do it in the service of liberation.

Align your healing with *power with* rather than *power over*. Financially
this means examining and then releasing any ideas of saviorism, and
embracing ideas of reparations, resource return, and mutual aid rather
than charity. One of the absolutely most helpful things that healing does
is change the way that you project your own unhealed and unfulfilled
self onto people and situations around you. When you are not on a
healing path, you are always seeking to fulfill unmet needs from your
past, and you will bring this to your activism, your parenting, your small

business, your friendships, and your romantic relationships. Once you stop projecting, you will be able to see people for who they really are, not for what emptiness they might fill for you. Bringing this to the realm of money is truly radical.

MINDFULNESS MOMENT

100 Percent Pure Love

Find a comfortable place to sit, breathe deeply, and settle into your body. Become aware of the tiny spark of life that was placed in you by Creator. You may visualize it as a tiny dot of glowing golden light the size of a sesame seed. Imagine this seed at your heart center or at your third eye, in the center of your forehead. Nothing can destroy it and nothing can blow it out. You possess a pure soul, given uniquely and perfectly to you.

When you feel comfortable and are in touch with the light within, chant this Hebrew prayer in your head or, preferably, out loud:

El-o-hai ney-sha-ma shena-ta-ta bi teh-horah hi.

This translates as "Creator, the soul and the breath that you have placed in me are pure."

This prayer is traditionally said upon waking up in the morning, and is an appreciation and acknowledgment of the breath of life that has been placed within our body.

Allow the vibration of the words to reverberate through every part of your body and spirit, healing and repairing the damage that shame has caused. Return to this meditation as an antidote to shame whenever needed.

BUILD NEW HABITS

Most of our behaviors are habits or reactions. Being intentional in the sphere of action means interrupting those instinctual moves and choosing our actions on purpose. Behavior is how you conduct yourself, the actions that you take in relation to yourself and your environs. Your behavior in turn has impact on your environment—the systems and organisms that surround you. So your behavior creates a loop, and acting intentionally also brings intentionally chosen energy to all aspects of your life.

We've done a lot of work in this journey of understanding our reactions, conscious and subconscious, voluntary and involuntary. In clearly seeing the mechanisms of our behavior, we get so much more opportunity to intervene and insert positive, self-loving, and self-esteem-building actions into our financial life. Often just seeing our reactions clearly is enough to shift the behavior. Let yourself have some ease and notice the ways that more healed financial actions may instinctively come through now that you have identified what they look like.

Going to the next level also means actively introducing new habits into your life. In order for habits to stick, you can't hold them at arm's length; you have to invite them inside your inner circle of concern. This means that your new habits should answer a want rather than a should. When you build from a place of desire rather than a place of guilt, you are going to see better results. Assess your strengths and incorporate them into your plan. What are you great at doing already? What is going well for you? Work off of that. If you're already having good luck with sitting down and looking at your finances once a month, add a savings transfer at that time, moving even $5 into an easy online investment account. What feels exciting and activating for you? If you're motivated by upgrading your living situation, use that to drive action in making some side income, searching for a better-paying job, or asking for a raise. Build off your knowledge, your experience, and your resilience rather than focusing on challenges or deficits.

Remember back to those intentions and affirmations from step 4. This is where setting goals comes in to complement that work. Goals are specific and actionable. They are how we get moving along in the direction we set by our intentions.

Make an action plan. Keep in mind that making change is big work, and give yourself compassion in the work you are doing. Large to-do lists and grandiose goals can become overwhelming, so break things down into actionable items and put them on a time line. Show care for yourself by making your plan realistic and respectful to you specifically. Set yourself up for success.

JOURNAL PROMPT

Level Up

What are some financial habits that you have noticed shifting over the time you've been reading this book? What new habits have formed with ease? Where do you feel a genuine and authentic pull to treat your finances more lovingly?

Piggyback new habits off of already established habits. Momentum is quite a force (cashing in my dad joke card now) and can help carry new habits into being. If you have a standing phone call with your bestie on Saturday morning, ask if they want to start incorporating a money check-in. If you always watch your TV show on Thursday after dinner, could you work on your bookkeeping at the same time? What about checking your bank account balances while you commute or have your morning tea? Look at what new habits you want to jump-start and see what you've already got going that could give them the boost they need.

Do not do this alone. Even you Scorpios and Capricorns out there who can't stand to ask for help need to allow someone in to support you. This can be an accountability buddy, a friend you trust to talk about what is happening in your financial life, a therapist who can hold you in uncovering your family of origin links to money, a mentor to talk to you about the business side of your industry, a bookkeeper, a past-life reader. There are so many ways to receive support! Naming the help that you need is powerful. When you vulnerably ask for the support you want and need, you give a gift not only to yourself but to the larger community web, as it gives permission to others to do the same. You deserve help and others want to give it. (As always, we're checking both entitlement born of privilege and negation of needs due to marginalization while we find our footing in this terrain.) Opening up your web of support is part of community care. Show up for extended community with the energy and resources you have to offer and then cast a wide net when naming what your needs are. Someone will have the right skill set, the time availability, and the follow-through to be a resource to you.

JOURNAL PROMPT

Team Spirit

What habits, knowledge, and qualities do you already possess that will help you on your journey to heal your finances? Who is on your team in achieving your financial goals? Who is cheering for you in this process?

THE VOID IS A PART
OF THE PROCESS

It's easy to let our concept of abundance get caught up with the way our brain thinks about capitalist economics. It is not easy to shift into other ways of thinking. When we demand that abundance occur on a time line, when we judge our own manifestation skills as lacking, or when we view our fallow periods as an abundance failure, we are getting caught up. Abundance is a part of the natural world, and thus it has cycles.

Abundance is about generation, creation, and growth. In nature, growth cycles also involve dying back, releasing parts that have served their purpose, letting those dead bits break down in the compost pile, and then regrowing in a new form out of the rich, dark, fertile soil. As any gardener who has planted in composted dirt knows, the beauty is that some of what sprouts will be the seeds you intentionally planted and some will be the rebirth of what died off. I always get some volunteer tomato and squash plants.

Your cycles of abundance will be the same. There are other parts of the growth and generation and productivity cycle besides the moment of harvest. Your fallow season is still generative. When nothing seems possible, when you have failed, when everything is collapsing around you, embrace the compost pile. Yes, it hurts to experience loss when pieces of our life die back or must be pruned. And it absolutely hurts like hell to have to sit still and get broken down. But these are times to just be, to just sit, to accept what needs to move on for future growth to occur. The time will come again to plant seeds of miracles in the fertile soil of your life. There is abundance in the void. The void is nothingness, but it is also infinite potential. Allow yourself to experience the full cycle, to be a part of the natural process of abundance, and harvest time will come again. I promise.

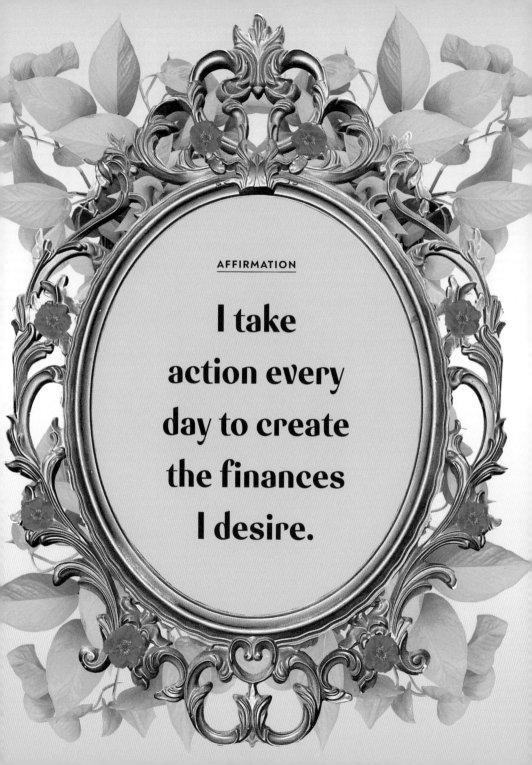

AFFIRMATION

I take action every day to create the finances I desire.

RITUAL

Manifestation

Set up a writing space that feels special, nourishing, and generative. Light a candle, burn some herbs, and settle in. Make sure you feel warm and secure.

Use nice paper—this may mean a journal or notebook that is significant to you, or paper that is high quality or pretty—and a special pen. Color magic can add extra impact: Athena Bahri (@crystalreikihealer on Instagram) suggests gold or yellow for positive thoughts and strength, green for wealth and growth, brown for earthly and material needs or security, red for ambition and motivation. Of course, do not let perfect be the enemy of good, and if you don't have, can't find the energy to gather, or can't afford the items I suggest, just grab any pen and paper!

Write down your top financial goal for the next one-year period of your life. Next, write an additional reflection on what will change in your life when you achieve this goal. For an extra-poignant connection between your personal energy and the paper, try to write the entire goal down without lifting your pen from the paper.

Write seven times "I will manifest" and then your goal. Seven represents an entire cycle of creation.

Use the next twelve lines to list the next twelve months, and then next to each, write what action step you need to take that month in order for your goal to come true within twelve months. Cocreate with the Universe.

Hold your paper between your palms and visualize your dream coming true. Imagine that the time has arrived to harvest the rewards of all your effort and striving. How do you feel? What do you see, hear, and taste?

Remember that all is not clear in the current moment. Wisdom develops over time, and your plan will need to shift and pivot as more information becomes clear. Be flexible and agile; listen to the wisdom that crosses your path as you strive toward your goals, and incorporate it into the plan. Ask for spiritual counsel from your deities, angels, ancestors, and spirits and trust that help is on its way. Listen to guidance on how to manifest your end game even if the advice is not what you would have assumed or preferred to hear. Know what you want, believe that you deserve it, and embrace support from your spiritual team.

Thank the Universe for receiving your prayer and follow through on the actions that will bring your dream to life.

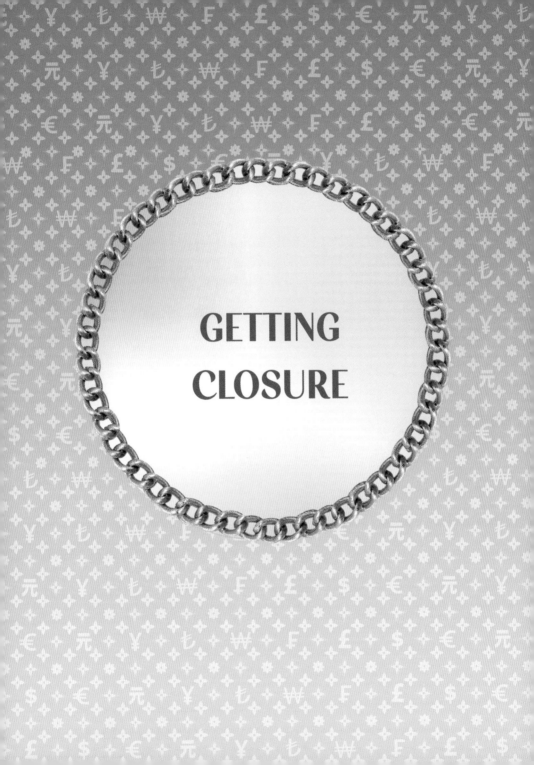

GETTING
CLOSURE

My babes! We did it!

Thank you so much for taking this journey with me. No road is more profoundly beautiful than the path toward healing. Beautiful and sometimes painful. Joyful and profound. Seeing and being seen, witnessing and being witnessed. Thank you for inviting me into one of your most intimate realms, the realm of money and survival. It is truly an honor to walk with you.

Thank you for showing up for yourself, for little you, for wounded you, for hopeful you, for aspiring you.

Thank you for doing this work to become self-loving. You're doing such a great job and I'm so proud of you.

When we come to a knotted-up place in our personal web, it feels messy and ugly; it is vulnerable and we feel out of control. We may be afraid of exposing the knots because we are afraid to be seen in our unevolved places. Let's support each other in the vulnerability of our evolution. Loudly evolve. Become different. Heal. All we can offer each other, and ourselves, is evidence that we will do the work. That we will not abandon the process of learning how to love better and be better stewards of this world. Hold yourself with deep compassion as you evolve.

We will forever be in a place of growth and process. Having to heal is not a by-product of existing; it is the entire work of existing—it is our one and only real job. We are always changing and becoming, always evolving, and always untangling our ancestral and inherited webs. We are forever learning liberation, forever unlearning the things that have served as oppressive agents inside of our bodies, the places where we have glossed over an experience out of a need to simply survive it. Let's go back for those parts of ourselves that have been left behind; let's gather them up and ask them what they need. Let's grapple with them. Let's promise never to abandon them again. Do not disown essential parts of yourself for the sake of relating. Take every moment of injury as an opportunity to choose healing rather than shame.